CONVERSATIONS WITH THE OTHER SIDE

⸔ ALSO BY SYLVIA BROWNE ⸕

BOOKS/CARD DECK

Adventures of a Psychic (with Antoinette May)
Astrology Through a Psychic's Eyes
Blessings from the Other Side
Contacting Your Spirit Guide (book and CD)
Heart and Soul card deck
A Journal of Love and Healing (with Nancy Dufresne)
Life on the Other Side (with Lindsay Harrison)
Meditations
The Other Side and Back (with Lindsay Harrison)
Past Lives, Future Healing (with Lindsay Harrison)
Prayers
Sylvia Browne's Book of Angels
Sylvia Browne's Book of Dreams
and . . .
My Life with Sylvia Browne (by Sylvia's son, Chris Dufresne)

The *Journey of the Soul* Series
(available individually or in a boxed set)

God, Creation, and Tools for Life (Book 1)
Soul's Perfection (Book 2)
The Nature of Good and Evil (Book 3)

AUDIOS PROGRAMS

Angels and Spirit Guides
Healing Your Body, Mind, and Soul
Life on the Other Side (audio book)
Making Contact with the Other Side
Meditations (also available as a CD program)
The Other Side of Life
Prayers (also available as a CD program)
Sylvia Browne's Book of Angels (also available as a CD program)
Sylvia Browne's Tools for Life

and . . . *The Sylvia Browne Newsletter* (bimonthly)

⸔ ⸔ ⸔ ⸕ ⸕ ⸕

All of the above titles—except the newsletter—are available at your local
bookstore or by visiting: Hay House USA: **www.hayhouse.com;** Hay House
Australia: **www.hayhouse.com.au;** Hay House UK: **www.hayhouse.co.uk**
Hay House South Africa: **orders@psdprom.co.za**

CONVERSATIONS WITH THE OTHER SIDE

Sylvia Browne

HAY HOUSE, INC.
Carlsbad, California
London • Sydney • Johannesburg
Vancouver • Hong Kong

Published and distributed in the United States by: Hay House, Inc., P.O. Box 5100, Carlsbad, CA 92018-5100 • *Phone:* (760) 431-7695 or (800) 654-5126 • *Fax:* (760) 431-6948 or (800) 650-5115 • www.hayhouse.com • **Published and distributed in Australia by:** Hay House Australia Ltd., 18/36 Ralph St., Alexandria NSW 2015 • *Phone:* 612-9669-4299 • *Fax:* 612-9669-4144 • www.hayhouse.com.au • **Published and Distributed in the United Kingdom by:** Hay House UK, Ltd. • Unit 202, Canalot Studios • 222 Kensal Rd., London W10 5BN • *Phone:* 44-20-8962-1230 • *Fax:* 44-20-8962-1239 • www.hayhouse.co.uk • **Published and Distributed in the Republic of South Africa by:** Hay House SA (Pty), Ltd., P.O. Box 990, Witkoppen 2068 • *Phone/Fax:* 2711-7012233 • orders@psdprom.co.za • **Distributed in Canada by:** Raincoast • 9050 Shaughnessy St., Vancouver, B.C. V6P 6E5 • *Phone:* (604) 323-7100 • *Fax:* (604) 323-2600

Editorial: Jill Kramer • *Design:* Julie Davison

Library of Congress Cataloging-in-Publication Data

Francine (Spirit)
    Conversations with the other side / [channelled] by Sylvia Browne.
        p. cm.
    ISBN 1-56170-718-X (tradepaper)
        1. Life—Miscellanea. 2. Future life—Miscellanea. 3. Reincarnation—Miscellanea.   4. Spirit writings. 5. Society of Novus Spiritus (Campbell, Calif.) I. Browne, Sylvia. II. Title.

BF1311.L4 F73 2002
133.9'3—dc21

                                                        00-040795

                        ISBN 1-56170-718-X

                    06 05 04 03 8 7 6 5
                    1st printing, March 2002
                    5th printing, August 2003

This book is dedicated
to Sylvia's grandmother,

Ada Coil,

who provided the wind
that filled the sail

§   §   §   §   §   §

§ CONTENTS §

Foreword

This book is a dissertation on life, afterlife, and reincarnation given by Sylvia Browne's spirit guide, Francine. Within these pages, you'll find a "gnostic" view of the world and the reason for life. As always, we encourage the reader to "take what you like and leave the rest behind." No single work can fully capture this enormous topic. We simply offer this book as a resting point in your lifelong search.

Our goal, and hopefully yours, too, is to stimulate your mind to seek God—however you wish. We don't intend to replace your belief system. Rather, we only hope to expand your view to include areas not yet explored. Each person will find and understand God in their own way. This book offers one path, among billions, to find God.

A wonderful writer, T. S. Eliot, said it well: "We shall not cease from exploration, and the end of all our exploring will be to arrive where we started and know the place for the first time."

— Sylvia Browne's editorial staff

§ Introduction by Francine §
(Sylvia's Spirit Guide)

There is information that I'll give you here that you've never heard from any other medium. Years ago, I couldn't have spoken to you as I will now because the world wasn't ready. It isn't that the information is new; it's as old as you are. I don't ask you to necessarily accept everything I say, but I'm convinced that in your heart of hearts, you'll be very aware of the truths spoken here. I'm going to discuss life, the reason for being, and the evolvement of the soul.

I want you to always keep a free and open mind; never feel that you're bound by guilt or social norms. Your life won't be "off track" if you go against the norm. Every person has their own track. I take a decidedly opposite view of any group that forces everyone into a certain staid belief. I only want—more than anything in this world with the help of God—to augment your curiosity and self-image, and help you take control of your life. It isn't important whether you're skeptical or not. More important, though, is the fact that you do believe. Even if there's a part of you that's skeptical, then even that curiosity in itself is a belief factor.

For years, we've been silenced by churches, society, and cultures. But if you're free-thinking, then you're not easily controlled. You should only be controlled by the God within, and no other force or pressure should be heeded. The God within will lead you down your own path of individuality toward your quest for knowledge and perfection.

§ § § § § §

❧ Part I ❧

LIFE: A REASON FOR BEING—
EVOLVEMENT OF THE SOUL

What is the purpose of living?

You're all messengers from God, sent to Earth to carry a message. But this message is encrypted, and you must decipher it within yourself. In other words, you carry a part of the emanation of the Divine. It's as though you're a scroll for the Word of God.

It's true that God exists without you, but *all* of you are a part of God. You will live forever, you have lived forever, and you will never be diminished or lost.

Spirituality means, in essence, finding yourself, finding the God within and without, and fighting the battle against negativity. You see, even if just one of you will go out into the world and show the light to others, then a "grayness" has turned bright. This is how you fight negativity, and it only takes a handful of you to accomplish a great deal.

Each one of you is here to evolve your soul. You've chosen to experience life in order to perfect more rapidly. You're evolving as a unique part of God, perfecting one aspect of Him and Her.[1] God experiences through His and Her creations. (In subsequent text, we'll refer to the "duality of God" using the pronouns *Him* or *His* for ease of reference.)

Start looking at life as something you must survive. It's something that can be fun, but it's also very tedious. As best you can, look at life as a school where bad food is served in the cafeteria and the teachers aren't always of the highest caliber. You'll make it through much better if you maintain a sense of humor.

Why does God need me for learning?

God, who is all-knowing, needs to experience His knowledge. From this need arose all of creation, which is the manifestation of God's emotion and intellect. Every facet of God can be found in His work. The perfect love between our Father and Mother became so great that it began to multiply onto itself, thus creating all of us. We've become the source that directly experiences emotions for God. We are, literally, a part of God. As such, anything we experience is also experienced directly by God. If we're having some type of difficulty, then God experiences it, too. If we discover a joyous facet of life, then God is also there.

It's true that God needs us to experience. Yet it's more correct to say that God *is* us, and thereby God does experience directly.

God has experiences over and above what humans do. This is true because God has *all* knowledge, whereas we have very little by comparison. For example, let's say that someone reads every book on how to build a boat, but they don't have any practical experience. As a result, they won't have the *total* understanding and feel of boating. Yet, just through the knowledge alone, they would experience the essence of boating, but not as much as by doing it firsthand. We're the sensing, feeling side of God's knowledge. Yet due to God's boundless wisdom, all experiences we have are of a far greater magnitude for God. God experiences through us, but is able to absorb much more than we can understand.

How should I live my life?

Self-acceptance and self-knowledge indicate that you're on track. Don't constantly attack yourself for being human and imperfect. Stop using phrases such as, "If I had done this . . ." or "If only . . ." These are useless and waste energy.

Take care of your body. Take pride in ownership. Don't deal in the past; this can be very debilitating. Don't become overly emotional over small things. If you do, then when the time comes for you to use that emotion for a larger purpose, you may feel that the "well has run dry." Intellect never runs as dry as emotions. When emotions run dry, a vacuum is created and it sets up an identity crisis. Then, you only feel like half of a person. But rejuvenation follows as you wait for the emotion to build back up again.

So, expend emotion wisely.

Can I change my path?

Everyone is very fearful of dissolving relationships. "How do I relate?" This is a common, worn-out question. "Relating" simply means to have a total love and intercourse with oneself—a constant communication. Those who have made the greatest strides are those who can communicate with themselves. If a relationship dissolves, it is simply time to move on. I don't mean to be glib about this because grief is also a part of life.

Do you know how often you create things? Throughout your life, you create "silk purses out of sows' ears." It's true that your eyes are blinded by what you first see in a person—a beautiful, sparkling gem of the euphoric part of the

Other Side. The union between a male and female is probably one of the most blessed and beautiful alliances of the universe. But don't devalue the union between friends, which is also very blessed and beautiful, even if it only lasts for a short time.

You alone are responsible for your destiny. Your life was fully planned by you prior to coming in. All of life's joys and sorrows were known beforehand. This is your chosen way to reach perfection. You can change your life only when the soul knows that it's time to move to a different experience. Ultimately, you'll experience everything you planned on, however painful, for the evolvement of your soul.

You never change your main path, just the little offshoots. The main highway always runs on a direct course. You can take "sightseeing" trips off to the side, but you'll always return to the main road. You view every single avenue and nuance of your path before you incarnate. You see all the shortcuts and detours, and what you would do with them. And you always ask yourself, "Will this add to my purpose?" That is why, if you start veering too far off course, depression sets in. The soul tries to remind you, through depression, that you're off track. Physical illness may even occur if you get too far off. For example, if you do one trying task, you may get a headache. If you do something else, you may get sick to your stomach. What someone else can handle, or struggle with, doesn't necessarily mean it's something you must also handle.

Everyone has their own path to take. Don't pattern yourself after someone else. You may endorse "hero worship" or great respect for someone, but your own path is unique.

How much "chance" is involved once we incarnate?

Each life is firmly set into place, regardless of the many directions it can take. As you travel on a highway, there are other roads that intersect and diverge. Your life is very much like this highway; you have one basic direction in which to travel. But sometimes there will be several roads to choose from, all of which will take you to your destination. If you turn in one direction, you may end up in the desert. So, regardless of the choices, you're still supposed to travel in one direction—your own road. That doesn't mean you can't take a detour or get lost, but most entities find their way back to the "main highway."

Everything you'll experience is planned. That's why there's so much counseling before you incarnate. You not only scan your own life, but you also scan major influences around you. So does everyone else. It becomes a gigantic network that you could never, ever fully absorb with your finite mind. The complexity of the many situations you'll encounter is mentally staggering. Many thousands of people are involved, and endless details must be implemented.

How firmly set is my future?

By coming into life, you essentially give up your free will. Once you've planned the life, you'll stay upon that path. Your free will operates *before* an incarnation. Afterwards, you're acting out your own destiny.

You're allowed to travel many different roads, but you must achieve your final goal. In other words, there are many ways to throw a dart, but it must hit the target.

You only have one destiny—to fulfill the mission you came in for. This is the overall first premise. Let's say you have the life theme of Justice.[2] You'll pick lives in which this theme can best be experienced. For example, if you were an Irishman in one life, you might then choose to be an Englishman in the next. This would give you the balance of justice. Justice is your main thrust. You may pick certain directions along the way to fulfill the Justice theme— maybe saving someone from being falsely imprisoned or even just giving a great speech. Your actions don't always have to be blatant. You don't have to beat a drum or carry banners. But the theme is always prevalent. This is the secret to your entire life—your theme. You'll reach the final destiny when you come to your last "exit point." Then you'll know, with all assuredness, that you've fulfilled your theme.

Many circumstances that arise in your life seem to happen by chance. Perhaps you weren't meant to break your foot, but there was a choice to do so. If you took this option, then you might have done it in order to get some rest. Or perhaps by going to the hospital, you could ensure harmony between two people who were fighting. In other words, you never get away from your theme. It will always rise up in front of you. To a person who isn't "justice-minded," the scenario of two people fighting wouldn't be something to act upon. But a person with a life theme of Justice would immediately become involved. They would say, "This *is* my business because it's bothering me." Thereby, even with this choice of circumstance, they're still fulfilling their goal.

Future lives are only planned within you. They're not written where I can read them. For this reason, commentary on future lives is nonsensical. However, therapy for past lives has a great deal of value.

Must I go through trauma and anxiety?

You decided to come to Earth because you wanted to perfect faster than other entities. That's a plus in your favor.

This is the last planet to be won for the sake of goodness. I don't want to give you the impression that everything on this planet is evil, but it has the thickest negativity of all worlds. Throughout the galaxy, Earth is known as "the marshes." All of you who have decided to come here had to be evolved enough to make it. This planet is the toughest schoolhouse that you'll ever experience.

Now, you may say, "I've fallen. I've stumbled." We expect that. We're never concerned with things that have to do with the flesh. The things we *are* concerned about, as most of you should also be, is the deliberate infliction of pain upon another individual. You may be surprised to learn that this happens very rarely. Most of the hurt inflicted by one individual on another is committed out of defense, or out of survival.

You get stuck in the marshes. Even your dreams are more bizarre on this planet. Earth is more surrealistic than any of the other planets. Medicine is far below par. Intelligence on the entire planet is far below par. This isn't negating any of you, however. It's just that when you come to Earth, there's a dulling of the mind. That's why so many times you may feel that knowledge is trying to get in, but something is blocking it. The atmospheric conditions are much thicker here.

People may say, "Oh, I couldn't have planned to die violently"; "Why did *this* happen?"; or "Why did *that* happen?"

As I've said many times before, you're only looking at a small portion of time. You can't see the truth of things from such a narrow vantage point. You can choose to die violently for a greater good. You who are left behind after a murder or death of a loved one are the only ones who must perfect that grief. The entity who died has already fulfilled their job as a catalyst for your grief. If you don't take *every* horrendous thing and turn it into a good, it's lost to you. The most evolved souls will take on a great deal of trauma in order to perfect more quickly. Rather than feel sorry for the person who has had a miserable life, as you often do, you should feel sorry for the one who has had an absolutely *marvelous* life. You are *all* going to get into scrapes. There's no way to avoid them when you're in the body.

But you don't have to get into any more scrapes than you allow to happen. Traumas don't come to you externally or from out of nowhere. They're preordained by *you* to happen. You may say, "I must be very masochistic." No, you aren't. You merely wanted to test your strength and see if you can endure.

What causes anxiety and depression?

Many of you suffer from stress and oppression. I want to be straightforward because if you know the reason why you feel the way you do, it's much easier to handle. If you develop an unknown malady, you become very fearful. But if a doctor specifically diagnoses your intestinal pain as simple bacterium, you're relieved to know it's treatable and not terminal. Inevitably, most of you suffer with life, and it *is* terminal. No one ever gives you a diagnosis for your pain. You feel alone and isolated by your feelings and anxieties. You aren't mentally ill, you're just tired—tired of wending from one part of the universe to another; and tired of trying to reach people who are not evolved enough to hear your words, believe their own healing force, or comprehend the power that resides in you. These tasks become very wearisome.

Don't settle for anything you can't understand. Everything you want to know may be difficult for the "finite" mind, but there's an answer. If no answer is given, there's a control factor. You were told in religions and secret societies that you weren't supposed to know or understand everything. This is foolishness. You *can* understand everything. Or essentially, you can certainly have the answers to everything. There's nothing too mysterious that you can't question or find an answer for. I'm not promising that you'll fully comprehend what you discover, but there will always be an answer.

You're already in a body that's heavy. Your body is a vehicle in space, in a world that's made up of antimatter.

You live in what we call a "static belt," an electrical belt. You're constantly being bombarded by your atmosphere. As a result, your body weighs heavily on you. Even your head weighs heavily upon your shoulders. Although you're used to this weight, it's very different from your eternal self. If you add all of this to the stress and difficulty of life, you'll be a miserable entity.

Competition, whether in social or technological areas, creates more stress. Those of you who came into this life and decided to enter "advanced" societies, wanted to perfect the fastest. You may say, "Well, what if I had been born in the slums of India? That would be worse." No, you wouldn't have had as much stress. You wouldn't have had the competition. You wouldn't have had the peer pressure. When life is merely dedicated to survival, it isn't as stressful as competition. In India, you're only competing from hand-to-mouth. It's certainly a difficult life, but not nearly as damaging to the soul.

I don't want to preach to you. I'm only concerned about the depression you endure, the weight problems you struggle with, and the stress you face. Many ask why they can't find happiness or access their "inner self." This is the result of dietary habits, stress, and futility in comprehending the meaning of life.

We're finding more and more people who *are* happy. However, some are standing amid their happiness and screaming, "Why can't I be happy?" Happiness means that you elevate your soul, you have everything you need, you're living, you're functioning, and you're working for God. This is happiness.

Why do I react so strongly to life situations?

Have you ever gone to the dentist for a teeth cleaning and then complained about it? Yet, you were there by choice and knew that the cleaning had to be done. To react to life situations is part of the plan. You're here to experience all of it. By venting your emotions, you can better handle such things. There's nothing wrong with complaining. I'm more worried about the person who never vents. I don't suggest that you should rage all the time, kicking and screaming. No one wants to be around a person who's emotionally out-of-balance.

You can't take the constant barrage of infringements upon yourself and not react. And I don't mean in a violent manner. Many times a person will close up or just not respond. For that person, this method works. Yet another person will have to vent their anger. Everyone is different. The tragedy is that, with religion, psychology, and culture, we try to make everyone homogenous— nice, quiet, organized, and controlled human beings.

Schools try to do this, too. Everyone has to be clean, quiet, and perfect. But what about the kids who want to vent their own personalities? Why are they held back? The same thing happens with adults. Why do people constantly put themselves in a position where they're prevented from being themselves? "I'm not allowed to say that," is the cry of many entities.

If you're in a position where you can't speak and act freely, you're not allowing yourself to grow. I don't necessarily mean at your job. You can't walk up to your boss and say, "Look, I think you're crazy." But if you have nowhere to vent, you'll get into a job and life situation where you're stagnant. Soon, you'll have a home situation in which you can't grow. Then eventually you'll discover that your car doesn't work! You may think the car problem is just a coincidence, but it's really a result of the pent-up frustrations that imprison you. Ultimately, you'll be saying, "My children aren't right, my husband isn't right, my job isn't right, and now my car isn't right."

People hide their true feelings because they fear they won't be loved unconditionally. "If I don't confine and suppress myself, then I won't be loved. So the more I suppress myself, the more everyone will think how marvelous I am." This misconception continues until the day arrives when *you* no longer think you're marvelous. Then everything begins to bother you.

How should I react to trauma?

It is the resistance to life that causes pain. All you really need is the total and complete knowledge that God never allows anybody to need or want. Each person chooses to be in a position of need for the perfection of their soul. And each person has the ability—the inner power—to change such situations.

Once the need for anything is removed, there's an "abundance." *The flow of life is a cardinal rule in the universe.* If you don't block the way, the way will carry you. This applies to every human being. It's the same thing with pain. Once it's experienced and acknowledged, then it can be handled. The fear of pain, or the fear that accompanies pain, is what is so intense. Similarly, it's the fear of life that leads to most of your problems.

I'm not suggesting, however, that you flow with the tide of the masses! You can be an individual. Thomas Edison, and other great people, were able to flow with their own tide. If you know anything about Albert Einstein, you're aware that he didn't let anybody bother him. He, too, led his own life.

Most of the problems that we see on your plane are created because you really push *against* life instead of going with it. There's a disciplined frame of mind that allows you to flow with the life stream. But it's so simplistic that most people negate it. In other words, if a bad relationship occurs, or a job is lost, or anything else unpleasant happens, you shouldn't worry and struggle over it. Rather, you respond by saying, "I'll ride this difficulty for as long as I can, and then I'll simply jump off and deal with another one." People literally harangue situations to death because they have what Sylvia calls a terminal "one-time" quality about everything. "If I lose this job, I won't get another one. If I lose this person, there will never be another like them." *Of course* there will be!

Even with the tragic loss of a child, there's still something that will take the child's place. Most of the time, people are trying so hard to keep from being uncomfortable, without grief and without want, that they create the very situation they're trying to avoid. They create an emotional vortex for themselves where they become needy, filled with frustration and worry.

Does it really matter if you move from one place to another? Similarly, our loved ones just moved back Home early. You'll eventually meet them again on the Other Side. It's very hard to explain to human beings that life has a great plan. Even though we talk exhaustively about the Other Side and how everything eventually evens itself out, the frustrations still mount. Allowing yourself to flow is part of centering the self.

For instance, some parents will say as their children get older, "I'm more patient now. I can handle my kids." But this isn't the case. Somewhere along the line they learned to flow, and that's really what patience is all about.

Discontent will only occur when you aren't flowing well enough with life. Do you realize that 99 percent of your fears never culminate? But if even one tiny part of something you fear comes true, you'll say, "I knew it!" Not only that, but this affirmation intensifies *all* of the fears you've ever had. You may even think you're psychic enough to know that everything you fear will come true. No human being suffers that much trauma. You may look around you and say, "But this person was murdered." Yes, they were, but chances are they crossed over very fast and are now Home. I'm not condoning murder; I'm just saying that such an atrocity is also part of the larger plan.

Let's look at life as a school again. Let's say a student in your classroom flunks out and is expelled. For a short time, everyone will react by saying: "Isn't that terrible? What happened to cause that?" Ten years from now, will this occurrence be significant? During your school days, do you remember any "bad" students? Where are those students now? Are they directly intertwined in your life? Are they affecting you now? Yet for a brief time, everyone said, "I'm so glad I'm not one of those bad students." Everything is transient. Everything is moving.

Is it permissible to get angry at people and situations?

Don't be so scrupulous about your thoughts. *Thoughts are things,* but realize that you're human. Know that you must vent your feelings. I told Sylvia sometime ago that anger is an inverted depression, and psychiatrists have known this truth for years. Anger is inverted because you can't just be who you are since you're afraid of disapproval. Yet, whom do you admire in life? You admire the eccentrics, those who do what they please. I don't mean the people who hurt everyone, but those who can live their life the way they want. If that's what it takes, then be eccentric.

Your words shouldn't be monitored. I don't mean that you may maliciously hurt someone; but if you ask God to help you speak only the truth, you don't have to worry about censoring your words. If someone misinterprets what you say and gets angry with you, that's really their problem concerning their own perfection. You always have a choice when listening to someone. Anger is self-inflicted by you. You may say, "This person made me angry." But that's not true. *You* made you angry. Or, "That person hurt me." No, *you* hurt you.

Many times we carry people on our backs because we think we're doing a good deed. If you carry a baby who raises its arms to you all of the time because it doesn't want to walk, then that child's legs will atrophy and they'll never walk. Haven't you then damaged that child with misguided kindness?

Jesus said, "Love your neighbor as yourself." Now, let me be more specific and try to release some of your guilt. You can't possibly like everyone, but because "love your neighbor" has been driven into you, you're convinced that it's wrong to dislike people. On the contrary, it's wrong *not* to dislike people. Let me tell you why. If you're going to like and care for every person (and I'm not speaking of love—we'll get into that later), there's something wrong with your personality. You're deficient as a whole person. A whole person has definite likes and dislikes, paths that they follow, paths that they don't follow. You must try to love everyone's soul and wish them the best, but you certainly don't have to like them or their actions. To associate with a person you intensely dislike is wrong. It diminishes that person and yourself. Many marriages, friendships, and family relationships often encompass people you can't tolerate. This causes you guilt, heartache, and stunts your spiritual growth; you're laboring so hard to be perfect that it colors everything.

Anger is probably one of the most positive motivators you possess, yet you're always told not to be angry. You *must* be angry when it comes to injustices. You *must* vent your righteous anger. You are sound of mind and know that you aren't going to be aggressive. There's a difference between aggression and anger. You develop so many ills because you invert anger, and most of it is anger toward yourself. When you invert your anger, you create a great overabundance of adrenalin, you develop a case of acid indigestion, and most likely you'll contract dysentery. You see, if you don't release your anger one way, you're going to release it in another.

People say, "I was so angry, I cried." Do you know why this happened? You couldn't let the anger out, so your tear ducts let loose. People also say, "I got so upset, I vomited." This is another way to physically release your anger. Why can't you turn to an individual and say, "That hurts my feelings. I don't like what you said"? You're afraid of being rejected. Isn't it better to feel rejected than to be dishonest about your feelings? Are you aware of the secondary effects of suppressing anger? You begin to isolate and ignore people, which leaves them wondering what's going on with you.

You have every right to remove yourself from a painful situation. Otherwise, it will stunt your spiritual growth. If you've spent a year or two with an individual and there's absolutely no improvement in your relationship, you're wasting your time if you go on any further.

Only *you* can judge how deep a hurt goes, how deeply you're affected by a situation, and how deeply you're injured by it. This is the only time you can make a judgment. How much does something bother you? Does it stunt your growth? Are you nonfunctional with it? Does it hurt you too much? If a relationship has overriding positive qualities; if an individual moves in and out of negativity and there are no bad feelings, or if you can neutralize your feelings, then the relationship is worth pursuing.

If you can't extricate yourself from an individual, then you should neutralize their impact on you. By neutralizing them, you insulate yourself so they can no longer hurt you. This process uses the objective part of yourself, so you don't subjectively translate a bad relationship as a personal rejection.

Don't get caught up in the tragic belief that you can change someone. Although some marriages are built on this belief, as are family relationships, you're ultimately building your house on a foundation of sand.

Is there a "proper" way to be?

One thing you must guard against is holding another person responsible for your needs. It not only drains you, but it drains the other person. It's like the old adage by Edwin Arlington Robinson: "Love must have wings to fly away from love, and to fly back again." The most enduring relationships in the world have survived in freedom.

The only reason you'll ever look at another person and say, "You make up my total life," is because there's a deficiency within you. This is a perfection scheme you need to overcome.

If you find that you're a person who doesn't like other people, you're in great turmoil. Not only is your world filled with people, but where you come from is filled with people. *The greatest thing that you will ever do in this life is to try to get along with other people.* This doesn't mean constantly giving out more than you wish to. It simply means being amiable. It's perfectly within everyone's right to show anger and fear. The problem with many psychologists is that they try to make you verbalize such things. There are some emotions that just can't be verbalized. Some emotions must be enacted, and there are others that, unfortunately, can't be accepted.

In other words, if you're tremendously frustrated, you shouldn't run screaming down a street. It's a pity in a way, because this action doesn't hurt anyone. Or if you were to lock yourself in a room and break things, this wouldn't hurt anyone either. You become so confined within your own body, in a vehicle that doesn't work exactly as it's supposed to, and you have a subconscious memory of a body free of heaviness and ills. These, in themselves, cause frustration. Do you know that Jesus didn't like everyone? He didn't like the Pharisees; he couldn't stand the

Sanhedrin; he couldn't tolerate the rulers of Rome; and yet he cared for all people. Do you understand this notion? It's impossible for you to walk around and truly love everybody. When you claim to do this, you have prostituted the word *love*.

You've used the word *love* so much that when it comes to truly loving and caring, you can't measure it anymore. Most of you, I can truly say, "like" and "care" for others. Very few incarnates know what true love is. This isn't because you're deficient; it's because on your plane of existence, it's nearly impossible to comprehend. Infatuation, experienced in those initial moments or months of a relationship, is probably the closest way to describe "love" on my side. But where I am, you must multiply this by 1,000. Once you get a slight hint of this feeling with a new partner or friend, you're constantly searching for it again. But as you get older and more weary, the less often it comes. Nevertheless, something must replace it; some deep inner peace and the knowledge that you're finishing out your time and on your way Home.

You may select partners and companions along the way; however, each of you falls into a state of isolation because of your physical body and the fact that you can't merge. We as spirit guides are probably closer to you than any human being could ever be.

Remember when you were first romantically and mind-lessly in love with someone? In this state of heightened euphoria, you wouldn't care if your car didn't start or you lost your job. Do you see what I mean? Even if you did care, it would be minimal. But let the infatuation wear off, and *then* your car won't start and you lose your job, and you'll be in the throes of despair! The only love affairs that last are those that you have with your God and yourself; and even the deep, abiding love that you have for the people around you. I'm talking about comforting love.

Infatuation in your world is wonderful, but it must be given lower precedence than comfort and companionship. People often make a commitment and then relinquish it because they're looking for that gigantic thrill. It doesn't happen often, nor does it last. People who search for that infatuation ultimately age before their time because their body can't sustain it; it's too intense. As you know, when you're infatuated, your heart races, you lose your appetite, your face flushes, you can't sleep, and even your blood pressure elevates. You couldn't sustain this state—you'd eventually die.

When we find one of you in a state of infatuation, we can actually see your aura sparkle and flare all over. Did you know that after infatuation, there's a gray period? If you work through it, then you'll usually turn a bright green or bright blue, which means rejuvenation or tranquility has taken place.

You are electrical beings and you're in control of this electricity. You should visualize your aura so it becomes more green or blue, or maybe even shades of green and blue. Your aura should also be confined close to the body, without flaring out. The best aura is one that is close to the body. You'll show two or three layers in your aura. When the aura is closer to the body, it will be white or light, almost like a silhouette. If your aura extends three to six inches out from your body, then you're in a very excited mood. When your electrical emanation reaches out about three or four feet, this is what we see during infatuation.

If you're constantly living in the past with what should have been or what was not, then you'll stunt your spiritual growth. If you're constantly wondering all the time about what people think of you, you'll stunt your growth. If you constantly stay with someone you dislike intensely because society rules that you must, you'll stunt your growth. Does it make you an uncaring, unfeeling human being if you do these things? Maybe society thinks so, but you must realize that, in actuality, you're alone and you're following your own individual path to get back to where you came from.

If I can only encourage you not to be obsessive about things such as tomorrow, next year, or money problems, then your life will be much easier. You may retort, "But I have to live." Yes, you do. But things are only going to be one way or the other. Believe me when I tell you that everyone survives the money worries, the business worries, and the love worries. So much needless energy is spent on worrying about things already predestined by you.

Money is a great deal like love. It's meant to be taken in and given out. If money is received and held onto, it doesn't reproduce. People become too concerned about materialistic holdings. I've talked to people constantly in private sessions and they ask me, "Am I too materialistic?" Almost every time, I've answered no. Very rarely have I seen a person, regardless of their holdings, houses, or cars, who I feel is truly caught up in material possessions. People *are* caught up in material matter by caring too much, in almost a self-conscious way, about what people think of them. *This* is being caught in matter. The solution is so simple. You care for the majority of the people and hope they care for you. If they don't, then there are others who will. This is the best mode of behavior. This is what makes you more spiritual.

You see, by quieting down the mind and knowing that God eventually—not only within but without—will take care of all things, you leave the door of communication open for us to enter. We can't get through when you're constantly filled with anxiety about money or a love affair. We can't seem to convince you to still your mind long enough for us to make contact. You can be simplistic yet very intellectual. This means you care for the smallest as well as the largest. It's a whole process of retraining your mind.

Be simplistic. Walk into your dwelling, whether it's an apartment or a house, close the door, and be grateful you have four walls and that they reflect you. Be thankful for a job that brings money in so you can eat and live, for friends around you, and for a beautiful country in which you can enjoy oceans or mountains.

I don't want to sound like those so-called gurus who want you to be so simplistic that you empty your mind. I've even been called very "Westernized." I find this label very strange because my philosophy is very Eastern. I'm considered Western, perhaps, because I believe in activation as well as passivity—*activation,* defined as doing something with yourself; and *passivity,* defined as letting life pull you.

I've also said this to Sylvia—don't struggle upstream, let the stream carry you. Fighting against life stunts spiritual growth because the path becomes harder. On the path you've chosen, try to avoid placing one rock after another in your way. Most of these stumbling blocks are created by you. Oh, yes, there are many types of stumbling blocks—periods of grief, periods of joy, periods of aloneness. But your frame of mind determines how well you'll get through them.

If every misstep you make is blatant, you can easily identify and stop them immediately. When you were young, all you had to do was put your finger in your nose and somebody would reprimand you, "That looks awful and disgusting." Then you stopped doing it. If everything you did was visible to the world and somebody would say, "That's disgusting," you'd stop doing it. You'd learn right away. In other words, you'd understand from the beginning that your actions were socially unacceptable. So, start acting in public the same way you would in private.

You should also recondition your mind, like you do with your body when you start swimming, running, or playing sports. You can tell when your body begins to get into shape. Similarly, every time you recognize one of your personal problems, say, "I don't like this about myself; therefore, I'll stop it." And I mean *immediately* correct it.

Reprogram yourself to acknowledge that you're not the negative part of your behavior. Most human beings only identify themselves with the negative. If you ask people to describe themselves, they'll immediately point out the negative because they're so fearful about stating their best attributes first. The most simplistic methods are the ones that are always overlooked.

What causes such diverse behavior in people?

Throughout all of your lifetimes, you've been inundated with the wrong information. When you go back into life after life, you're brainwashed into another type of "normal." You're deluged by all types of moral behavior, commandments, church rules, and law. So it becomes terribly difficult to figure out what's right.

One's upbringing in an incarnate state makes a person obsessive. If there's anyone reading this book who thinks they're not obsessive, I can prove otherwise. Knowing obsession exists, yet still giving yourself a sense of freedom, is marvelous. Everyone can reach this state.

When a extremely rigid society exists, eventually it reverts to extreme amoral conditions. This can be quite beneficial because if you've been conservative in one life, you can look forward to another one that will be liberal.

What causes psychological disorders?

This is the only planet where cancer exists. There's no other planet with this disease. The more people are engulfed with negativity, the more self-hate they inflict upon themselves and each other, and the more cancer there is. If you stop hating yourself, you won't get cancer. I don't mean that you dislike some things about yourself. I mean you *really* hate yourself, or really hate your life. What I'm saying to you, in essence, is that you have a very high peak to climb. But more important, I believe that you'll all reach the top. You might not think you're going to make it, but you will.

Multiple personalities are an entirely different matter. Most of the cases—99.9 percent—occur because a person can't figure out which life they're in. In other words, subconscious memories of your past lives seep into the conscious thoughts of your present life. This is known as a "bleed through" of your many lives and can overwhelm your mind and totally disrupt your life.

Is it better to be an active or passive person?

We've never seen anyone attain an immense thrust of spirituality by being passive. I'm not against any religion or sect except the ones that manipulate people's minds or create fear. The ones we find utterly useless are those that require years of being locked away and passively chanting. Spirituality is an ongoing, thrusting force. You'd never hear about Jesus sitting cross-legged and chanting for hours at a time. Instead, he was out among the masses—talking, speaking, activating, healing, and preaching. This doesn't mean that you'll turn into an evangelist. The greatest teacher and preacher you'll ever become will be for yourself.

Do extroverts evolve more quickly than introverts?

Yes, they do, but not false extroverts. Extroverts are people who genuinely commit to God to be as out-going as they can be, and believe beyond a doubt that God will take care of them—inside and out. In this commitment, God will provide infused knowledge and a direction for life. Then, they can let life have its way with them.

Is the strain of living worth the effort?

In humanity, we find great pathos and humor. The only message I want to get through to you is this: Stop trying to invent and reinvent yourself. The consciousness movement is a marvelous thing. Yet, there's an extremely *hard wall* you're going to hit. You'll be so busy making your emotions "flat," and fashioning yourself into such a perfect entity, that no one will want to live with you.

If you do nothing else but survive your life and deal with the density of your own body—wading and surviving through it—then you've accomplished something for God and your soul.

Can we ever hope to improve the world?

The planet Earth, due to its stupidity and negative cycles, must return ad infinitum. Once other planets experience the lesson of inquisitions and horrifying events, these atrocities no longer take place. Your planet, however, has a tendency to repeat such flagrancy. Ironically, this is very beneficial because without these negative pressures, you wouldn't have accelerated as quickly as you did. So when you look at each other and know you're all God's messengers, then you're one step closer to improving the world.

There are a limited number of years left for Earth. In this time, the spiritual movement must rise so that the planet can be "saved." There's no such thing as "lost." Let's just use the word *saved* in this context as "when everybody perfects their soul." If you can't reach this level, your efforts are wasted. Isn't this why so many of you decided to come in? Evidently, this is why the population is overflowing. It's because everyone wants to find truth. The real truth, of course, is in the very core of their being. Unfortunately, most people discover only part-truths. These individuals live in fear of life, which is why cults form with often disastrous results.

Life's negative aspects exist for the sake of perfecting your soul. Racial barriers, for instance, are set up to test the soul. Challenges such as being short, tall, ugly, beautiful . . . allow each person an environment to perfect.

If we're unable to cope with life, can we take an early exit?

You may never try to take your life prematurely. It only forces you to return and face the same circumstances again. And if that isn't a deterrent to suicide, I don't know what is.

Once you're in life, you're supposed to stay in it. If you commit suicide—and this is a known truth—you'll have to come back to the same geographical location, the same type of parents, the same type of marriage, the same financial disaster, or whatever events influenced your early exit. You'll go through *exactly* the same episodes again.

A common misconception about suicide is thinking, *Next time, I'll be more prepared and I'll handle things better.* But that's not the case because we push you back immediately. There's no rest and no time for revival. Remember this analogy: If a child runs away from school, they're admonished and sent back immediately. It's the same for an entity: They're continually sent back until they learn to stay in.

Most advanced souls wouldn't commit suicide. This doesn't mean that the soul that takes its life is bad, however. The more advanced soul may contemplate it but would never do it. It may even enter their mind, "My beloved has gone and I want to go with them," but there's always something—the wisdom of the soul—that holds them back.

On the other hand, you can be on track and take an "exit point." Remember, an exit point is never considered a type of suicide. An exit has already been set up, whereas a suicide derails you from your path.

How do we know when we're "on track"?

You're on track when you simply feel good about yourself. Regardless of any adversity in your path, you begin to realize that you can spiritually handle it. At times you may feel derailed, but there's an inner faith and glow that brings you back to this peaceful state. It's an intuitive understanding that you're okay; it's a love of yourself.

While on track, you'll experience heightened awareness, sensitivity, and the ability to hear guides or feel their presence. You may also receive imprints of their thoughts.

People are a reliable barometer for how well you're evolving. If you feel that no one likes you or you don't have any friends, most of the time this is *your* fault. Sometimes you put yourself in such a negative place that you can't see that you actually *do* have friends. You could very well be so hateful and cruel that no one wants to be around you. Here, I'd recommend that an adjustment be made.

Often, we hear people crying out, "No one loves me!" If you're unloved, there's a distinct possibility that you're *unlovable*. People work hard on being loved. But they don't strive hard enough in the art of loving. If your only thrust in life is just to *be loved*, then you may find that your soul "goes begging." But if your aim is *to love*, then you'll never find your soul in want.

If you cry, "Poor, insignificant me," you won't find much sympathy in this world. When you pass over to my side, you'll have to overcome all hostility and belligerence. Nothing destroys the soul more than carrying vindictive feelings. Not only that, it's also tiresome for others to be around you.

If life is forever, why does humankind have such a fear of death?

You'll find that those who fear death are more rooted in the materialistic world. Fear of death blocks the knowledge that life continues. Have you noticed, these days, how every-thing must be accomplished *now?* You must be successful, you must be wealthy, you must be beautiful . . . people rec-ognize subconsciously that this world has only a short time left and they must complete their perfection now.

We can even say that a fear of life creates a fear of death. Life, as you know it, is a very terminal condition. The only real "death" is to leave the Other Side for an incar-nation—where your reality is stripped away and replaced by an inferior existence. Here, another fear arises: "Will I ever get back to my real self?" "I want the true me, where is the true me?" In this life, you can't completely peel away the various faces you wear. Even your body is a false front and not the true self.

Have you ever lived in a house that you were afraid to give up because you thought you wouldn't find another one? Or have you gone on a long trip and then come back and said, "I forgot how good home feels"? These are the things you worry about. "I'm in a false dwelling, it's arid; I'm separated from others by a body; I can't pull another person into myself; I'm isolated from everyone here." If you can understand what's operating, then you'll avoid the fear of annihilation. When you pass over, all such fears are wiped away. Here, true memory bursts upon you at the very moment of your passing, and your soul breathes a sigh of relief: "That's over, and I'm going Home."

Can we choose to incarnate in another time with fewer problems?

Don't get any fancy ideas that you may go Home before your time. If you try an unscheduled passing, you'll be immediately reincarnated. There aren't any passages other than your preordained exit points.

You can choose any time frame to incarnate. But you'll never escape the problems of life, because those, too, are chosen by you. You'll experience everything your soul has ordained for itself.

What methods will help us survive through severe stress?

Deep breathing and meditation are the best ways to survive stress. Mental fatigue is possibly the worst type of stress. The only way to relieve it is to project your mind to a mountain or a seashore. A few minutes of this type of meditation can relieve stress and burdens. Amazingly enough, you can't relieve mental fatigue with sleep. The mind needs a diversion for relief.

The more you discover advanced spiritually, the more you realize how life is only a passing shadow. You certainly need to concentrate on your love life, your business, and your health, because these are all part of life. They're so transient, it's like a short stay at school. You may not like the dormitory or the meals, but you'll graduate. I guarantee it. No one has ever regressed.

Don't stay in situations you can't tolerate because they hinder your spiritual growth. People justify this by saying that if they leave a relationship, they may hurt someone else. My question is: Are you hurting them by leaving, or are you causing them more pain by staying? I'm not advocating the breakup of marriages or partnerships, but too often, people linger endlessly in a relationship thinking that: *If I leave, what will they do without me?* Well, they may just live!

Here's something you can do for yourself and others. On my side, we call it "sounding." *Sounding* is, at best, a very nebulous word. It relates to the internal workings of one soul touching another soul. Sounding is what we call the mental intuitiveness of one soul reaching out to another. It's the act of sending out premeditated waves of love and warmth. This may seem simple, but it's as if you feel or sense the body of another person. Sounding is probably the most psychic way to tell where you can find another person's spiritual core.

If you send out these loving waves and you find they're blocked—continue to send them. These waves can relate to your job, your marriage, and even to your own internal negativity. Another way to prevent blocking is to imagine that there's a glowing entity, your own spirit guide standing in front of you—rejuvenating you especially in the solar plexus area. They shall send loving waves to you.

I want to give you several meditations to practice. If you're going to accelerate, you should do each one of these every day. They don't have to be long or laborious. If you can put up with seemingly endless things—telephone conversations with people you don't want to hear from, television programs you don't care about watching—there's no excuse to avoid these meditations.

People can spend endless hours preparing their clothes or hair or sales sheets for the following workday, but will allot little time for spirituality. Let's make these following meditations some of those "have to" tasks.

THE SHELL MEDITATION

I want you to begin by visualizing yourself inside an egg. This is almost like going back into the womb. Picture yourself inside this egg and let the shell represents the "white light" of the Holy Spirit. Visualize yourself sitting inside the egg, touching its walls. Feel how secure and warm it is. This egg is somewhat transparent so you can see light shining through it, diffused light. The more deeply you feel this shell around you, the better the meditation will be. Let the egg completely enclose you. Then say, "I'm the most important person in the universe," which, of course, is the truth. The egg you are in is the universe.

Continue with this affirmation: "I can be quiet, I can be still, and I can be peaceful. I can be whole, I can be helpful, and none of the world's negativity can penetrate this shell. Here, I am my best friend and companion." Now, allow the shell to crack just a bit. This process symbolizes birth. Do not allow any fear to attach onto the word shell. *Unfortunately, we condemn people in shells. Yet it is a very positive act to "shell up" for a while because in doing so, you find a great deal of love. Your own love will bounce off of this emanation of the Holy Spirit, thus returning to you. In essence, the shell and the egg symbolize the resurrection of Jesus, and new life. If it's done faithfully, this meditation creates a type of rebirth each time you practice it. In other words, this exercise offers you a new beginning:* "I don't know if I like myself so I'll shell up and try it again. Each time I crack the shell, I'm giving birth to myself. It's new, it's bright, it's shiny, and it's beautiful."

THE RAFT MEDITATION

I want you to use what we call the "raft." Visualize yourself in water. It's dark, the wind is blowing, and you're very frightened. Let yourself experience a mild phobic reaction. If you're afraid of water, practice this meditation anyway. Feel the waves, feel the darkness, and feel the aloneness. All of a sudden from this deep darkness, you see the clouds begin to disperse and find yourself bathed in moonlight. You're floundering, you're coughing, you're wet, and you're cold. After the clouds disappear, you notice a raft nearby. You've never seen this raft before. As soon as you spot it, you feel an overwhelming sense of security. You begin to swim toward it. Astonishingly, you actually see yourself on the raft. You may question, "If I'm in the water, how can I be on the raft at the same time?" The "you" in the water is the phobic, fearful you—the emotional, floundering, scared, frightened you. The "you" on the raft is the smiling, confident you.

Ultimately, the goal is to bring the two together. The confident "you" reaches down and pulls the frightened "you" into the raft. Lo and behold, the frightened "you" merges with the stable "you." Now, imagine that the water, the darkness, the fear, and the cold all represent the negativity you've had to experience in your life. When you've gone through despair, grief, and fear, you feel like you've been abandoned. If you're working through a tragic job, a bad marriage, or a difficult family situation, throw yourself into the water and fight your way back to the confident "you" waiting on the raft. Remember, when it becomes easy for the frightened "you" to merge with the confident "you," this doesn't mean that you have "arrived." You'll still experience grief, suffering, and negativity many times in your life; and you'll be thrown back into the water with yourself. Use this meditation and make sure that you always merge with your confident self. In other words, make the cold, frightened self disappear so that only the beautiful, shining, smiling self remains.

§ § §

The greatest meditations you can practice will involve being near or in the water. These are the most effective since water is a symbol of birth, rebirth, baptism, and cleansing. The more you can use water in your visualization techniques—even a creek or stream works well—the better. We won't get into the psychological aspects now, but water also means *mother*; however, we're totally out of that facet at present. We're beyond psychological overtones, elevated up into the higher self now, the upper consciousness.

THE STREAM OF LIFE MEDITATION

While sitting, turn your hands with palms up in your lap. This will help you receive energy from your guides. Surround yourself with the brilliant color of emerald green. Now, close your eyes. You'll begin to feel a very warm glow and gentle pulsation in the solar plexus. Become very aware of your body. Now, you'll experience a strength and a slight pressure in the center of your body. Visualize the color green. If you feel that your body needs to adjust, try to control it so that you'll remain still. You're not going "deeper"; you're actually advancing "higher" into your upper mind-soul.

While in this higher state, visualize yourself in a small boat on a stream—the stream is about 15 feet wide, ample for a small boat. The boat is not an elaborate one. In fact, you won't even need oars. Just sit very quietly and let the current carry you. As you're drifting, begin to sense the tremendous emanation of the emerald green. To intensify this color, envision the foliage around you gleaming a brilliant green hue with overhanging branches.

As you continue drifting, notice how the foliage, like life, gets thicker and starts to slow you down. The current is not as strong now, and the weather is beginning to get somewhat humid and uncomfortable, just as life becomes troublesome and irritating. Nevertheless, keep your mood stable. Say this affirmation: "I will survive this. I will not become irritable, cranky, disrupted, or let prejudice besiege me. I will not allow these negatives into my life." At times, the boat will get hung up on the outstretched branches. You long for more rapid travel, a smoother path with the wind against your face. Yet, as in life, you're held back by these obstacles. If you wish, you may fight these branches or try to push them out of your way, but they're too thick. Gradually, a strong gust of wind thrusts the boat back into motion. The branches that you feared would hurt you, scratch you all the more when you try to interfere. However, the higher branches pass over you, and those along the shore just scrape the boat. As you begin moving again, you're free from the snags, and without any effort by you—as in life—you're back on your path.

When you hit obstructions in your life, this doesn't mean that you must be passive. Most of the time you fight to avoid your own destiny. You battle hurdles, but in time, you'll be delivered from them. The cuts and bruises you endure are to no avail. So, let yourself be active because you're moving in this boat. You watch, you look, you're pleased, you're happy. And you're content to go with the flow of life because it will take you where it must—without any interference from you. You put yourself on automatic pilot before you ever come into this life, and the only reason you don't fulfill the total mission is because you've meddled in the plan. You will complete this mission, either in this life or the next. Just try to live instead of interfering.

§ § §

When chronic pain occurs, it begins to permanently "groove in." That's why doctors are at such a loss about the causes of pain. It originates in the neurological system, and it doesn't always shut down after the inflammation or malady has ceased. It just keeps sending signals. The nervous system has been so traumatized that it tricks itself into believing that the pain still exists even after it's gone. Your mind has to reprogram itself and say, "I've received the signal. The trauma no longer exists. I want you to stop." The more you can create your own anesthetic, the better off you'll be. Repeat this affirmation: *"I've intercepted the pain, I can now produce my own anesthetic."* It's like talking to your own God, and saying, "That's enough. The pain is too deep, and I don't want to put up with it anymore!" Just make sure that you don't stop any other valid signal coming through, except in the problem area.

When you give someone advice—and all human beings are filled with advice—avoid the tendency to speak to yourself through another person. Try to be objective. This is the most spiritual road you can follow. Whenever someone asks you for an opinion, don't internalize it. Rather, try to put yourself in that person's place. This is a very spiritual modification of human nature.

Learn to be more self-centered and more caring toward yourself. Reward yourself more. For one week, do everything that you wish to do—just for you. I guarantee that by the end of the week you'll not only be nurturing yourself, but you'll be doing more for other people than you've ever done before. The reward of self takes very little effort, but once accomplished, causes so much love to emanate. There's no such thing as true selfishness—there is only fear, and fear causes you to be introverted and closed off. The word *selfish* has no meaning.

THE LABORATORY TECHNIQUE

I want to teach you a very powerful method
for dealing with any problems, whether they are

mental or physical. This is a general healing technique that can be used by anyone. We call it the "Laboratory." It's a place that you construct in your mind, where you can go to receive healing, counseling, or help with any problem. As you know, on the Other Side, thoughts are things. And when you mentally construct your own Lab, we can see it, go there with you, and help you. But you must first create the reality for us.

You create the Lab with your mind. Here's the basic layout of the area you should visualize. In your mind's eye, build a rectangular room. The far wall will be an open space where you have a nice view of a water scene, which will add power to the healing. The other three walls are light green—this is also to signify healing. In the center of the room, imagine a table large enough for you to lie on. Give the table a little character—adding carvings or some other type of ornamentation. The more detail you give to this room, the stronger its existence will be. Construct the table and walls out of any material that pleases you. The room shouldn't be too stark, so place a few things around you—chairs, artwork, and other items that you find familiar and comfortable. Now, imagine a stained-glass window in the open wall. This window can be designed as you like, but the colors must be very bright. Fashion the window with large blocks or bands of blue, purple, gold, and green.

Once you've constructed the Lab, mentally walk into it. The best time to do this is at night, as you're going to sleep. But please, complete this meditation before falling asleep or the Lab will disappear. Of course, you could use someone else's room, but try to construct your own. When you enter the Lab, stand in front of the glass window—then allow each of the color beams to penetrate your mind and body. The color blue *furnishes tranquility to the soul and spirit; the color* purple *provides for increased spirituality and awareness; the color* gold *offers heightened dignity and intellect; and the color* green *promotes healing. Allow these brilliant colors to encompass you in warmth and happiness. Try to visualize each of the colors as they enter you and cleanse your soul. Now, ask for the white light of the Holy Spirit to surround you and make you well. Feel yourself becoming whole, with a new sensation of stability, power, and control.*

At this time, go to the table and lie down, still wrapped in the glow of God's love. Invite master teachers and doctors to work on a particular area of your body. You must specify the area of concern and target only one problem area during each session. Concurrently, you can ask to be relieved of emotional and mental pressures. Surrender completely into their hands, as they are directly from God. Once you've gotten to the table, you may fall asleep. This is okay because the room has already been created, you've asked for help, and specified the problem. The table itself has an anesthetic quality.

Use the Lab for any problems in your life. You may even bring a loved one here. First, create the setting, then mentally put them into the white light, call on the Holy Spirit, visualize them on the table, and ask for the master teachers to help with their problem. Now, believe me when I tell you this: The Laboratory technique is one of the most miraculous meditations you'll ever use. There's no limit to what you can do in the Lab. The only barrier you may encounter is a person who doesn't want help. If you don't see any results when helping someone, then obviously, they don't want help. You can't interfere with another person's choices.

THE TEMPLE OF QUIET

Here is another meditation to help you with other problems that come up. For these, we'll go to "The Temple of Quiet." This is a place on the Other Side, a very ornate and beautiful temple shaped like an octagon. To get there, you can mentally ask to be taken by your spirit guide. You can also practice this meditation at night just as you begin to fall asleep.

As you approach the temple, walk up a few steps and enter it. The floor appears to be marble, but as you advance toward the center of the room, each block you step on emits a beam of light that shines directly into you. It's really quite lovely. Some of the emanating colors include shades of pink, mauve, blue, and green. When you reach the middle of the room, you may ask that a certain problem be resolved. At this time, an octagonal crystal set in the wall across from you will emit a beam of light into your third eye. When this occurs, the problem comes to life in front of you, enacted in a three-dimensional movie. When you view it, you'll see all of the options open to you to solve your dilemma.

You can use The Temple of Quiet for any problems in personal relationships, job situations, tests, or financial matters. It can be used for anything that you're concerned about. You can also tailor the end results in any way you want. But remember, view all of your options first.

For example, if you lose your job, what's the next option? It may be just getting a better job. If you can't get along with someone, examine all of the options enacted before you. Then you can choose the one best suited for you. The Temple of Quiet is probably one of the most beneficial meditations, and it's not difficult to do.

Actually, you practice this technique all the time in your mind—with hypothetical situations. You get so accustomed to seeing things outside of yourself, and that's why when you're trapped in a physical body, it's so hard to muddle through your own thought processes. In other words, let's say that I'm in the temple now and a beam of light is shining into me. A screen would appear before my eyes and I'd see myself acting out a certain situation. If I didn't like the scenario, I could change its focus and direct it to other options. Do you see what I'm saying? The Temple of Quiet is very functional in working out problems, although you may ask, "What's the worst that could happen?" Surprisingly, the worst you can anticipate can be reprogrammed into something better. So, if you don't like the outcome of a problem, you can reconstruct the characters and work out the solution any way you want for your own evolvement. This phrase is vital—"for your own evolvement." Keep it intact and integrate it within yourself. You're not going to do anything to disturb someone else's life, because everyone is linked up.

§ § § § § §

[1]The duality of God is discussed later.

[2]A complete description of all of the life themes can be found in *Soul's Perfection*—Book 2 of Sylvia's *Journey of the Soul* series.

⚘ Part II ⚘

AFTERLIFE: THE OTHER SIDE

For centuries, humankind has wondered whether or not there's an afterlife. In this uncertainty, people have seen fit to use various words and phrases—religious or otherwise—to describe this state. Depending upon one's belief system, descriptions can range from the well-known terms, *Heaven* and *Nirvana,* to more ancient monikers, such as *Mt. Olympus.* Within the Society of Novus Spiritus, we call the afterlife and its environs the "Other Side." In the following pages, you'll read in detail about the Other Side—its function, lifestyle, and population—in other words, its total environment and purpose.

Those of you who have been dogmatically programmed into traditional beliefs and descriptions of the afterlife will be quite surprised by the information presented here. The free-thinkers will be amazed by certain aspects and content, and those of you who don't have any belief in the afterlife might just find one here.

You'll most certainly gain something from this information. So, keep an open mind and take only what feels right for you. Some of you will avidly absorb everything and find peace and love therein; and then again, some of you will digest bits and pieces that fit into your belief structure. I believe, however, that even the most skeptical person will see and recognize the truth and logic behind the Other Side.

§ § ê

What is the Other Side?

The Other Side is simply "another dimension." You can all relate to the three-dimensional environment you live in, called Earth. In fact, except for those who have experienced some sort of "paranormal phenomena," you only have a conscious memory of Earth. You accept it as reality because you can see, touch, and hear all of the events that take place in your world. Consequently, you feel somewhat secure in this view of reality and rarely bother to question God, the afterlife, or existence itself. Life seems fairly simple, whereas religion (and its multitude of beliefs) is very complex.

Your soul is in the dark, but not because your five senses failed you. You're really looking for the truth; but which person, church, or organization has the answer? The dilemma is believing in something without any tangible proof. This isn't easy, as evidenced by the preponderance of various religions, philosophies, and scientific theories.

The possibility of another dimension is not a new thought by any means. Philosophers and mystics have expounded on this for centuries. Scientists have also gotten into the act, so to speak, with their theories of parallel dimensions and alternate universes at the other end of a black hole. For the moment, I ask that you set aside any confusing theories and listen to logic.

You know that you exist because your five senses tell you so. Descartes said it well, "I think; therefore I am." If you accept this reality and your existence, then logic tells you that you have a finite existence at best because of your limited life span. You then have to ask, "Is that all there is?" Logic again dictates the obvious answer—no. The reason is simple: It would be the greatest joke ever played on humankind. To say that your only existence is your short life on this Earth, especially with all of its inequities, is ridiculous. Life on Earth is not at all equal. Some of you live a long time; others exist only a short while. Some of you are poor; others have considerable wealth. Some of you have a racial background that is more subject to discrimination than others, and the list goes on and on. Clearly, to define existence as merely your life span on Earth doesn't make any sense.

So, where's the rest of your existence? Again, you must use logic for your answer. If you can't perceive the remainder of your existence with your five senses, then it must be beyond the realm of your sense perception.

The Other Side is, indeed, beyond the normal sensory perception of humankind. It's another dimension at a higher frequency of matter. In actuality, *it is reality!* Think logically for a moment and consider how 100 years compares to an eternity. It's like a drop of water in a very large ocean. If logic dictates *this* comparison, then it must also mandate that the vast majority of your existence isn't on the Earth plane. And when you aren't on the Earth plane, you, like me, are in a place we call Home. It's a paradise, it's a heaven—it's the ultimate reality of existence. I'm the living, and you, in essence, are the dead, because you're living in a time-bound state of unreality.

Please don't be upset by this, because eventually all of you will come Home and exist in the true reality that I'm in now—when you've completed your purpose on Earth. You may not be able to fully comprehend the fact that you now exist in a state of unreality, but let me assure you that when you pass over to my side, it all becomes very clear. At that time, you'll have a complete resurgence of all of your memory and senses uniting in the true reality. On your Earth plane, you're at a disadvantage because you don't have all of your faculties available to you, as you would when you exist on the Other Side. There's a reason for this. It would be too painful and unbearable if you could fully recall Home.

Most entities, at one time or another, schedule a physical life to experience negativity. There is no negativity on the Other Side—the true reality of existence. Negativity exists on your Earth plane, but since it's a part of knowledge, almost all of God's creations choose to garner that wisdom to augment the evolvement of their soul. The purpose of life is to accumulate knowledge and experience for God, and you never stop doing this, not even on the Other Side.

To summarize: Your true existence is in another dimension we call the Other Side. This dimension has a higher frequency of matter, which is beyond the realm of your five senses. It's a dimension where you reside for eternity, except for your sojourns to a plane of unreality (like Earth), where you temporarily dwell to experience and learn for the evolvement of your soul. The Other Side is your *real* Home.

Where is the Other Side?

The Other Side is a dimension that exists nearly "on top of" the dimension you're residing in now. There are variants, however, since the Other Side is subject to different laws of physics from your plane. The Earth plane is temporary and contains negative energy, so it's actually what you might call antimatter. The energy and matter on the Other Side is *true* matter.

The Other Side is superimposed on your plane, but located approximately three feet higher. This is one reason why those who have seen "spirits" or "ghosts" see them floating a little above your ground level. Basically, the Earth plane and the Other Side share the same "space." But due to the higher vibrational frequency of the Other Side, you can't sense and perceive its existence. On the other hand, you're like "ghosts" in our world—since our sensory levels are more developed, we perceive you much easier than you sense us. We just need to concentrate a little and activate our senses to a sharper pitch so we can see you clearly and "look into you."

Despite our close proximity to the Earth plane, the Other Side is not a complete reproduction of your material world. Everything that is beautiful on your plane—picturesque mountains, trees, flowers, rivers, and so on—is replicated on our plane in basically the same locations. However, we don't duplicate changes created by humans unless they're of great beauty. Although we have large bodies of water on the Other Side, our oceans are not as immense as yours. Much of the oceans' surface on your plane is land on ours.

This brings us to another very important point. Since the laws of physics vary on the Other Side, we have more room to reside here. Let me explain this so you can understand. Without changing our size, we're able to fill a nine-by-twelve-foot room with hundreds of people. Our physical laws allow us to do this without shrinking to a microscopic size, because space on our plane is entirely different. So, even if we have more entities who exist on our plane, we have much more space and aren't in the least bit crowded. This also applies to land, open space, bodies of water, buildings, and all material things.

Up until now, I've talked about the location of the Other Side in relation to your planet. Earth, however, isn't the only inhabited planet in the universe. There are millions of planets like yours where entities of various shapes and sizes exist and every inhabited planet has its own Other Side. In essence, each Other Side is a beautiful replica of its particular planet, and is located in the same dimension—so we travel frequently among them as we choose.

Whenever we travel to other areas of the universe, we proceed by code numbers. The universe is divided into many diverse areas, and this system makes it easier to pinpoint locations. To cover such a vast realm, code numbers are assigned to different sections within sections so that a particular locale can be found.

For example, if I want to go to the area of the Crab Nebula, I might say I'd like to go to XL-16 and "wish" myself there. In an instant, I arrive. We can teleport ourselves immediately by thought alone, but it's hard to explain this phenomenon unless you can see it. We also have a large information board where we can check code numbers and locations to direct our travel to unfamiliar places in the universe. I, myself, have never been to the outer regions, although I know many entities who have.

The convenience of travel has established effective communication among the various Other Sides of the inhabited planets. Overall, this augments knowledge, as discoveries are freely exchanged. For the purpose of your understanding, however, I'll confine my discussions in the following text to the Other Side of the planet Earth. Nevertheless, keep in mind that most Other Sides on various planets operate similarly.

Can you describe the Other Side?

The beauty of the Other Side is so glorious that you might term it "unbelievable." I can assure you, however, that it's even better than I describe. If you can picture the most beautiful thing you've ever seen and then multiply it by 100—then you might be close to imagining the beauty and composition of the Other Side. The colors of the Other Side are indescribable, especially since you don't have this type of color on your plane. They're brighter; with more hues, richness, and depth than any color you've ever seen in any picture, flower, or cloth. The greens are green-green, reds are red-red, and so on. It's very hard to portray them unless you've experienced them.

Colors, especially, are evident in nature. Our flowers are absolutely gorgeous and much larger than those on your plane. Our grass is dense and soft, our trees greener than green, and it's all lush and vibrant. All the natural wonders exist on our side—mountains, rivers, trees, flowers, grass, rocks, lakes, and seashores, which combine into great vistas of incredible beauty. Certain areas such as these are also uninhabited so that we may enjoy the wildness and freedom of nature.

All animals on the Earth plane, from an elephant to a household pet, can be found on the Other Side. The difference, however, is that they're friendly and sociable. You'll see a lion cavorting with a gazelle, rather than chasing it. There's no loss of life or predatory hunting of one animal by another. Enemies within the animal kingdom on your plane are outright friendly on ours. The only living creatures absent on our side are those that are irritants and ecosystem necessities. Insects, such as the common housefly, ant, or mosquito, don't exist—and neither do any pests, including rats and snails. Only animals that are beautiful or that add joy to our side are duplicated.

It might interest you to know that your pets, which reside on your plane, proceed to the Other Side when they die. If you've loved a dog or a cat, they'll be waiting for you when you come back Home. My dear Sylvia has a huge domain where all of her pets, which she has gathered throughout her incarnations, are waiting (and they are a considerable number); and when she comes Home, there's always a big reunion.

Several humanmade structures, if captivating, are duplicated on the Other Side. We have buildings representing every type of architecture, although most of these reflect the classic Greek and Roman periods. We have huge forums where we listen to lectures and view the arts, tremendous libraries and research centers where we gather knowledge, as well as individual homes and smaller buildings for either residing or general use. We have exquisite fountains and plazas, courtyards and parks, as well as gardens and meditation areas. Even the descriptions of Utopia wouldn't be enough to portray the splendor and efficiency of my side. It is indeed a paradise!

It might also interest you to know that there are areas on the Other Side that cater to an entity's fondness for a certain lifestyle. For example, let's say a person had many lives in a particular period of history, such as medieval times, and they grew to enjoy that era. There's an area on my side that exclusively depicts the architecture, music, art, and work of this time. An entity may choose to live in this medieval environment—with all of its castles, villages, social habits, dress, and all things pertaining to that period. Similar environments exist for nearly every cultural period in the history of humankind.

Here's additional information about the Other Side: First of all, we don't have seasons. The temperature is a constant 72 degrees without fluctuation. This is very comfortable for us—not too hot or too cold, and it allows us flexibility to dress however we want without having to worry about the weather.

Second, we don't have a sun. The Other Side is bathed in a somewhat rose-hued light, which is constant and amplifies beauty. There's also continuous light, since we don't have what you call night. Ultimately, there isn't any darkness on the Other Side, only light and beauty.

Do we have a body on the Other Side?

Yes, we definitely have a body. I realize that some of your religions profess that there is no body or, at best, only an ethereal, intangible mass on the Other Side—but the truth is, you have a definite human body with shape and substance. Believe it or not, your body on the Other Side is even more real than the one you now have on your plane.

Here are several facts you're going to enjoy about your appearance on the Other Side: First of all, you and only you choose your body and its features. You decide which physical attributes you want—from the color of your hair to your height and weight. You choose whether or not you're slim, stocky, or somewhat plump. As an entity, you were created to be a certain sexual gender, so while you can change your body's appearance whenever you want, you can't change your sexual makeup. You choose your facial features, the color of your eyes and skin, and your figure and physique.

In addition, you can pick any imperfection for your body. This is a symbolic gesture to show that God's creations aren't as perfect as He is. This blemish may be a small scar, a white streak in the hair, or anything else that visually indicates a slight imperfection.

Another fact you'll enjoy: Your body doesn't require any sustenance—there's no need to eat, drink, or sleep. Most of us on my side only eat or drink as a tradition or custom for a social event. We don't sleep, but at times, we'll recline and meditate, or just relax. Without this need to consume, there's more time to learn, work, play, and enjoy our existence to the fullest. If a person *does* decide to eat, the food is usually tasteless—therefore, the act of eating for taste is pointless.

On the Other Side, your body is almost an exact replica of its composition here on Earth. It has a heart, lungs, liver, gall bladder, and so forth, but they're located on the opposite side of your body on the Earth plane. These organs have no function, but are a symbolic imitation of your Earthly body.

Is there a government on the Other Side?

We don't have a form of government, per se, but we do have a hierarchy. This is made up of a Council of elders, and then in descending order: archetypes, spirit guides, sixth-level entities, fifth-level entities, and so on. Before you get confused with all of these names and terms, let me expound on each one:

Elders are special creations who never incarnated. They have a very wise and beautiful Godlike love for all creation. As spokespersons for the Godhead, at least in a verbalized form, these elders bestow much information. They're humanoid in appearance, and instead of residing on any particular "level," they all walk with each other. They're wise, loving, and offer help to everyone. Unlike the rest of us, they take on the appearance of old men, with either gray or white hair and/or beards. Their wisdom is vast, and when needed, they're called upon to enact any policies or edicts.

Archetypes are also humanoid in form (without any sexual distinction), but are a completely different creation from the majority of entities who reside on the Other Side. They all look alike, almost like androids in human form; they all communicate telepathically with each other—but they don't communicate with us. It's not that they don't respond to us, but they're comparable to deaf-mutes—they have their own way of expressing themselves.

Archetypes are very bright entities and seem to glow with an energy that no one else possesses. At times, when you look at an archetype for an extended period of time, your eyes will react as if a flashbulb went off in front of them. The elders say that the purpose of the archetypes is to provide the purest love and protection for those on your plane, as well as ours. No one really knows how many of them exist, but when help is needed, thousands respond.

Archetypes are very powerful creations, and spirit guides use them frequently to help those they mentor on Earth. In your Bible, they've been called archangels. Due to their brightness and energy, they've been observed in your dimension and have even been mistaken for an apparition of Jesus. Not too much is known about them, so they're still a mystery to us—but the love and protection they've given us is not.

Spirit guides such as myself perform additional duties, such as communicating on your plane through mediums and/or psychics in various means. It takes many of your years to function in this manner (what we call a "control"), whereas everyone else operates as a spirit guide at one time or another. This communication is verbalized in several ways: through a medium who is in a trance (my method), manifesting physical phenomena through a physical medium, channeling energy through a psychic healer, channeling verbalization through a clairaudient medium (which I also do), and feeding strong impressions through a channeling medium. All of these practices take years of instruction, and if not conducted properly, can considerably harm a psychic or medium.

To understand the hierarchy of fifth- and sixth-level entities, I must elaborate on the seven levels of delineation on the Other Side. These levels are set up for the purpose of categorizing and organizing groups of entities according to their experience and vocation. They aren't levels of evolvement.

The first and second levels are for orientation, where entities who have just passed over from your plane reside temporarily. (These levels will be explained later.)

The third level is for all entities who choose a simpler, more rural lifestyle. These entities elect to work with animals, agriculture, and craftsmanship.

Fourth-level entities are a little more diversified, pursuing such aesthetic fields as art, writing, and crafts.

Fifth-level entities assist in orientations. Some are counselors, and others are controls—cultivating such areas as business, medicine, science, and related studies.

Sixth-level entities are organizers, teachers, orators, philosophers, and leaders.

Consequently, fifth- and sixth-level entities oftentimes become supervisors, managers, or leaders in various types of vocational endeavors. Due to the experience needed on these levels, entities take on even more responsibility as heads of research projects and orientation centers.

Seventh-level entities choose to go back into the Godhead, and therefore, reside on the Other Side for a short time. Few entities select this level since it requires the loss of your individuality and personality, as the energy of their creation returns to the Godhead. Entities who choose this level are usually very spiritual and evolved, for their love of God is so intense that they wish to be absorbed back into Him.

If our hierarchy is a form of government, it would most likely resemble a pure form of the ancient Greek democracy—complete interaction with everyone on my side, and the power for all to act or contribute if they so choose. Since there are no egos on the Other Side, our hierarchy rules with complete love and harmony—wanting the best for every individual, as well as for the whole.

Do all levels reside together?

Regardless of what level we choose to live in, we all reside in the same dimension. There are areas on my side where the populace is predominantly on the same level—for convenience, and lifestyle or vocational purposes.

While there are seven continents on your Earth plane, we have seven corresponding areas on the Other Side. Each of these is divided into 4 sections or quadrants, totaling 28 quadrants in seven different areas. Each quadrant has a main purpose of endeavor, and entities who contribute to these efforts reside there to share similar interests and/or vocations, and are also of the same level.

For example, in what you call North America, there are four quadrants. Quadrant one is basically very pastoral, populated with many animals, while research is conducted in husbandry and agriculture. It's inhabited by approximately 80 percent of the third-level entities and 20 percent of the fourth-, fifth-, and sixth-level entities.

Quadrant two is an industrialized area for research on new methods of production and design. It's inhabited by approximately 60 percent of the third-level entities, 30 percent of the fourth-level entities, and the remaining 10 percent is a combination of the fifth- and sixth-level entities.

Quadrant three is an aesthetic area, since so much art and beauty is created there. It's inhabited by approximately 80 percent of the fourth-level entities, 15 percent of the fifth-level entities, and the remainder comprise third- and sixth-level entities.

Quadrant four is the scientific domain for medical and scientific work. It's occupied by approximately 40 percent of the fifth-level entities, 40 percent of the sixth-level entities, and the remaining 20 percent contain third- and fourth-level entities.

It should be noted that all of the levels are equal, only distinguished by an entity's experience and vocation. Usually, the higher-level entities have more incarnations in life. They've visited the Earth plane more often, and hence, have gained more experience with negativity and all that your planet has to offer.

Do we work on the Other Side?

All created entities work on the Other Side. The word *work* is probably an inappropriate term in this case, since we all thoroughly enjoy our chosen field of work. Unlike your plane, where you work in order to feed, clothe, and support a family, we work because we enjoy it and can gain more knowledge about God, our Creator.

You'll be interested to learn that *all* knowledge that is accumulated on your Earth plane—from new discoveries and inventions to rediscovering ancient knowledge, was first accessed on my plane. This wisdom, gained from our work and research, is then transferred onto your plane in several ways—usually by implanting it into the brain of a researcher, scientist, or philosopher. Inventions, medical cures, new scientific theories, and discoveries are *all* transmitted from our plane for your benefit and use. Even such things as music, art, and new designs are implanted into individuals on your plane.

In general, we embrace several interests or hobbies in addition to our work. One of us may be an avid physicist, for example; and yet love to sail, write, ride a horse, or play a sport such as jai alai. Since we don't have any time references such as your hours and minutes—these exist only on your plane—we have plenty of free time to pursue any interests.

Without any sense of time on the Other Side, it's sometimes difficult to relate to your timetable. If you live to be 100 years old on your plane, you've aged only a few short weeks here. This is hard to explain because we don't measure the passage of time in any manner; we can only offer this analogy to help you understand.

When your loved ones pass over to the Other Side, they have a very difficult time leaving you behind on your plane. Although you'll be with them shortly, they know that you have to go through several trials and tribulations. They also recognize, however, that you'll be Home soon—safe and sound. Therefore, they can't get too upset over any difficulties you may go through—whether it be pain, suffering, or grief, because they know they'll see you soon, even if you have years left to live on your plane.

Let's say that one of your children cuts their finger on a thorn. You may be sympathetic while they're in pain, but you know the wound will heal and they'll function normally in a very short time. You can't get too upset over such trivial matters. This is the primary reason why controls such as myself have to go through such intensive training. Otherwise, we wouldn't be able to "relate" to your human problems. In a sense, we have to become almost humanly familiar with your plane and its nega-tive impact—however minor—on created entities. We have to learn to become sympathetic in order to com-municate effectively on your Earth plane—through a medium such as Sylvia.

So, don't be upset if a dear loved one passed over and you can't feel their presence or experience "communica-tion from beyond the grave." They're probably very involved in their work and only waiting for the short period when you return Home.

Do we have normal human functions on the Other Side?

We function very much like you do on your plane, with the exception of several positive differences. As stated ear-lier, we don't have to eat, drink, or sleep. Also, we don't have bowel movements of any kind, or any physical break-downs within the body or mind.

We have all of the five senses that exist on your plane, but they're greatly augmented. We can hear, taste (if we so choose), feel, talk, and see much better than on your plane. We never get tired, weary, or injured in any way.

Mentally and physically, we feel 100 times better than you do, even if you've never felt better in your life.

What abilities do we have on the Other Side that we don't have here?

Limitations on the body and mind differ from your plane to mine. Entities on the Other Side communicate telepathically for the most part, especially in small groups. In larger social gatherings, the verbal word is used so there is no confusion.

We also have the ability to bilocate on the Other Side. This means that we can visit someone or someplace and still continue to do our work. We concentrate deeply, and mentally project ourselves to that different locale, while we focus on being where we are. We can do this fairly easily, and many entities can bilocate to even more places for purposes of assistance. If necessary, Jesus can literally bilocate himself to millions of places.

In addition, we contain within ourselves all the wisdom open to us. All of our experiences are readily remembered and stored as knowledge—from all of our incarnations, as well as from the eons of learning and pro-gression we achieved while on the Other Side. Our total experience is known to us here, whereas the greatest bulk of your knowledge is blocked in your subconscious on the Earth plane.

Any knowledge we wish to access is available to us through the Akashic Records, which contain all of the wis-dom—past, present, and future—for your planet Earth and the creations that reside on its Other Side. Each inhabited planet has its own Akashic Records, which are indigenous to that particular planet and its Other Side.

Do we keep our identities and personalities?

All of you keep your basic identities and personalities—your individuality—when you're on the Other Side. The only exceptions are those who choose the seventh level and are absorbed back into the Godhead. The hardest thing for you to realize is that your personality and individual-ity act as a composite of all of your experiences—those from the Other Side as well as those from when you incar-nated in various lives.

Your experiences, whether good or bad, influence you as a person. Your actions, as well as the events you encounter, help create your personality and determine how you'll react in a given situation. You've lived in various locales throughout the world in past lives, and the experiences you collected while in those lives tailor your personality and individual identity *today*. This is one reason why hypnotic regression therapy can be so effective in solving psychological and physical problems you may have.

When you're on my side, your personality doesn't change; it works at its optimum level. Imagine that you're in the most joyful period of your life—with your personality at its peak, exuding charm and happiness. Take this feeling and magnify it by 100, and you'll get an indication of how your personality works *all of the time* on the Other Side.

What about people we don't like? Do we suddenly like everybody?

Likes and dislikes are a part of our individual personality, and they're directly attributed to our own experience. If we don't care for another person, it's usually because our experience with that person (or someone like them), has been negative. Dislike is not created into an entity; it must be formed from our own experience.

On the Other Side, our awareness is open to the fullest. We actually see why people treated us poorly, whether it was because they were under too much pressure, or the event was a learning experience for the soul. With this knowledge, our outlook is very different than it would be on the Earth plane. For the most part, we don't have any "dislike" on the Other Side. We love all of the souls of creation because they're a part of God, as we are.

There have been many cases when relationships don't work out on our side, but this doesn't mean that these individuals hate each other. They still love the soul but choose not to associate with each other. This is, of course, the manifestation of individuality. Each and every entity in creation has a choice to associate with whomever they want. We all have our close friends, those we socialize with more frequently or confide in. That's the purpose of individual personality and desire. I know of no one who hates or intensely dislikes another entity on my side—there's just too much love and harmony here.

The main reason for this love and harmony is the lack of ego. There's no competition on the Other Side. Everyone works together for the common good. Pride and jealousy just don't exist. This is due to the awareness and total recall of the knowledge that each of us retains in our super-conscious. We all know the purpose and reason for exis-tence—to love, and obtain knowledge for and about God.

You'll never find entities fighting with each other, whether verbally or physically. If there's a debate on a particular subject and someone gets angry, all entities in the vicinity will immediately become aware of this anger via the emanation of energy within that entity's aura. Then they'll rush to that entity to calm them down and return them to immediate awareness and reason. This is what's so marvelous about the Other Side—we all help each other to become more positive and loving—and with an envi-ronment free from negativity, it's very easy to do.

Are there social activities on the Other Side?

We have numerous social activities on the Other Side. There are so many that they literally cater to each and every entity. There's dancing and music in large ballrooms and auditoriums, lectures and debates on almost any subject, shows and galleries on every type of art that has ever been created, science shows and exhibits, sports events and regattas, fairs and exhibitions from other planets, fashion and design shows, and the list goes on. Whether a person wants to just view these events or actually be a participant, is, of course, up to the individual entity.

In addition to events of magnitude, there are many smaller activities taking place. We might want to listen to some chamber music, go to a dance, or visit a spa or vacation spot and enjoy outdoor activities such as archery or horseback riding. There are many places to fish (catch and release, of course); swim; sail; hike; mountain climb; or do whatever we'd like. There's no hunting, however, since nothing can be destroyed on the Other Side, nor would we wish to do so.

There are many athletic activities here. Most are non-contact sports, because no one feels the need for aggression. Sports such as jai alai, handball, and tennis are very popular; as well as sailing, swimming, and diving. Other sports include canoeing, rowing, hiking, equestrian activities, gymnastics, track and field, bowling, golf, and skiing. (The snow won't melt even at 72 degrees!) Almost any noncontact sport imaginable is played on the Other Side.

Other social activities include hobbies such as cooking. Even though food has little taste and is not necessary for our existence, gourmet chefs still like to cook and will participate in shows periodically; as will craftspeople, artists, and so forth.

Individual entities or couples are constantly throwing parties for their friends. This is one occasion when we might indulge in a little food and drink—not necessarily for the taste, but for the social atmosphere.

When we come Home to the Other Side, we find ourselves hard-pressed not to engage in some sort of social activity. Although we don't have to participate, most do. I myself am what you might call a "party girl." I love parties and dances, and I attend them regularly when invited. Sylvia always jokes that when I'm not around her (another guide stands in, so to speak), I'm off to another party. I do love them, as most entities do.

What can someone do for all eternity?

We work, socialize, learn, and enjoy our existence. It's interesting to note here that we're all 30 years old on the Other Side. This is the perfect age because we have a good combination of maturity and youth. Only the elders take on the appearance of being older to project their wisdom and learning.

None of us on the Other Side consider eternity to be long or drawn out, because time really doesn't exist for us. We're too busy to think of such things anyway. We're all blissfully happy, considering it an absolutely joyous blessing that we can exist in this manner, and we continue to learn about and exist with our Creator in a paradise-like setting.

Do we have houses on the Other Side?

Those who choose to do so can have a house on the Other Side. Entities who have soulmates (a form of marriage) live in individual houses. Many others live in dormitory-like structures similar to apartments with single rooms, or larger quarters where groups can reside. Since we don't need to sleep, we prefer this type of residence due to the social opportunities.

The houses where individual entities live can be of any design and style of architecture. Among the most popular are: Tudor, Georgian, and Greco-Roman, as well as contemporary designs. Many are elaborately furnished, while others are more rustic and simplistic. Many exhibit a multitude of glass windows and doors, while others are completely open. Every house is distinct because residents usually design them to fit their own desires and specifications.

The construction of buildings on the Other Side is handled in two ways. Some choose the conventional manner where carpenters, woodworkers, and artisans—who enjoy this kind of work—build the house. The other method isn't possible on your plane: Entities actually construct a building using only the energy of thought. Let's say we want to construct a new forum. The site will be selected, and several architects will outline the contours of the building using only their thoughts and ideas. If you could view this process, you'd see actual lines forming in midair, almost as if the architect was drawing these lines on a drafting table. By chance, if they don't like what they see, they can always erase the "energy" lines and start again.

Once this blueprint is complete, a group of entities gathers together and produce the materials for the building—walls, roof, windows, interior finishing—all in wood, or whatever substances are called for. All of this is done through concentrated thought processes that transform into real matter.

We essentially follow the same process to maintain our own appearance. If we decide to change how we look, we merely focus on changing our appearance, and we can instantaneously change, for example, from a blonde with blue eyes to a brunette with brown eyes. We do this from time to time according to our desires.

Is there marriage on the Other Side?

Since we live many lives on your Earth plane, we may have several husbands and/or wives. Let's say that an entity lived 20 lives. They might very well have 20 different spouses. On the Other Side, an entity has a soulmate, which is very similar to being married, only this relationship lasts for an eternity.

When we were created by the Godhead, we were intrinsically whole for the most part. I say "for the most part," because a soulmate is actually the created "other half" of ourselves. If an individual is created as a male entity, then a female entity is created to be the complement or "other half" of this individual—establishing, in two entities, the ultimate duality of male and female. Not all entities are created for this duality—some are created for the purpose of experiencing "singularity"—but the vast majority have a soulmate. A soulmate is a created entity who unites with another entity when both have determined that the time is right for this dual relationship to occur. It is, in essence, a marriage for eternity.

Usually, soulmates exist singularly until they've completed their own chosen level of experience and evolvement. Once they've completed their training, they come together and exist in a marriage as soulmates. This bond can take eons depending upon the individuals involved. As I said earlier, some entities have already gone through this process of learning and are now together, while others are still in the evolving stages. When the time is right, they almost always come together. An entity may or may not have a soulmate, depending upon whether they're a singular creation or they've reached the "time" of their marriage.

"Kindred souls" are those who have a very deep love for each other. Most of us have numerous kindred souls, but only one soulmate. For example, if we have a deep, loving friendship with someone in this life, it's probable that we're kindred souls on the Other Side. All of our close friends and "significant others" on the Other Side are kindred souls.

You may ask if there's sexual activity on the Other Side. Yes, there is a form of sexual relationship, which we call "merging." Merging is difficult to explain because it can be sexual or nonsexual, and you don't have anything like it on your plane. It's the act in which one's soul actually merges with, or comes together with, another entity's soul. In "sexual merging," the process starts out like the sexual act on your plane, but then the bodies actually coexist together, completely merged and fused.

Sexual merging results in the most intense of "orgasms," but it's tough to describe because you can't experience it on the Earth plane. If you can imagine the most intense and pleasurable orgasm that you've ever had and multiply it by 100, then you might come close to what sexual merging feels like on my side. This orgasm is also much longer than on your plane. If you can fathom an orgasm that lasts several hours, this may be a good indication of the length of an orgasm on the Other Side.

Sexual merging is acceptable and available to all entities. You must understand that there's no moral judgment for this act between nonsoulmates because it's done in the purest intent—love. Morality on the Other Side doesn't exist, simply because negativity doesn't exist. There's no such thing as "poor morals," because all entities are loving, don't have egos, and would never harm another entity in any way. This might shock those who live by high moral and religious standards, but your mode of life on the Earth plane is surrounded by negativity—while life on the Other Side is loving, peaceful, and completely blessed in every way. We don't have morality issues simply because there's no need for them.

Nonsexual merging, on the other hand, is the act in which the soul of one entity on my plane enters into another, and experiences the total essence of that person: mind, body, and soul. It's very intense and pleasurable. This process isn't sexual in any way, but occurs on a cerebral level, creating a mental high that's indescribable. Generally speaking, everyone on the Other Side has, at one time or another, participated in nonsexual merging.

Soulmates come together in the traditional way. The male entity will "propose" a union to the female entity.

If she accepts, and both are at their desired level of evolvement, they then go to the Council and ask for their blessing. Once this is done, the couple is sanctified and begin their life as soulmates on my plane. Choosing a soulmate always originates with the male entity. Although this may sound chauvinistic, it's a tradition we uphold. The female has the right to refuse or defer the offer in all cases. At times, more than one male may ask a particular female to be their soulmate. This circumstance is very rare, however, and never leads to any violence or bad feelings, as the female accepts whomever she wants.

Soulmates generally choose to live in a house together. This doesn't diminish, however, any of their prior social customs, activities, or friendships. Many soulmates live very happily doing things together, while others may want to pursue their own interests in a singular manner for a portion of their time. Either way is acceptable.

Can we see God or Jesus on the Other Side?

God is always present on our side, but not in bodily form. The presence of our Father and Mother is so powerful that it exudes through every pore of our body and every cell of our being. Our Father and Mother constantly communicate with all on the Other Side through mental infusion and love. The energy of God's love is a true manifestation on our side and is constantly present. There isn't a moment of existence on my side when we don't feel God's presence.

We're all bathed in God's energy of love and mental infusion every day, and there's a method that we can use to "speak" or "communicate" with God. Each quadrant has a designated area where an entity may go and speak directly to, and be confronted with, a portion of God's energy and presence—suitable for direct communication. This method is called "going behind the seventh level," and it is, in essence, the energy of all entities who have chosen to go to the seventh level.

Since all of us are a portion of God's energy and contain a small measure of His knowledge, many entities who have chosen to go to the seventh level encompass a great deal of Divine knowledge. All of this knowledge is combined with the concerted presence of God.

I myself have "gone behind the seventh level" several times, and it's an unforgettable experience. When I'm there,

I find myself in a space of mistlike clouds swirling around me. The energy of God is paramount, and the strength of His presence is overpowering. I can see and hear what seems to be millions of faces within this mass, and I can communicate and receive answers verbally or telepathically. Some entities choose not to go behind the seventh level simply because the energy is so powerful that it can be disconcerting—and even uncomfortable. The emanation of God's power is so strong that some entities can't handle it very well. The elders go continually for direct communication with the Godhead, but most entities refrain because there's really no need to go.

I've been told that certain created entities in the upper levels have communicated with God in a bodily form. This is only possible for specially created and powerful entities, such as Jesus.

Jesus does exist on my side in bodily form. His power and goodness are constant, and he's always a reminder that God's love is perfect. He walks among us and often talks with entities, interacting with all who approach him. Since he can divide himself into infinite locations, he's present at any time. You might notice him in serious and loving discussions with a group of entities by a fountain, find him walking on a hill with one or two entities conferring about philosophy, or see him laughing uproariously after someone has told a joke.

Jesus is not a morbid or suffering person by any means. He has a fantastic sense of humor, he loves to have a good time at a party or get-together, yet he can counsel or answer questions for anyone in need. Most of his counseling focuses on philosophy, or how to choose a theme for an incarnation. The bulk of his time is spent just being there for all of us, and personifying the epitome of God's creation.

What is the purpose of negativity?

While the Other Side is the eternal Home for all of us, many choose to incarnate on the Earth plane to experience negativity. Inasmuch as negativity is an aspect of knowledge, we incarnate on a negative plane to gain that knowledge, because without it, we'd be missing the total scope of all wisdom.

It's much easier to be positive in a perfect environment (such as the Other Side) without the burden of negativity. Most of us, however, test the strength and "mettle" of our souls to gain experience and knowledge about evil. This wisdom is needed for an accurate perspective of our true reality—the Other Side.

For example, how can we really appreciate and know joy unless we've experienced sorrow? How can our emotions relate to something evil, sad, or negative unless we've personally experienced that? Without knowing about the "black," we'd never appreciate (and perhaps take for granted) the "white."

One question I'm asked most often is: "If evil exists, doesn't that mean that a part of God is evil?" The answer is a resounding no! Certainly, God has the knowledge of evil and negativity, but that doesn't make Him evil or negative. In actuality, the "creations" of God cause and perpetuate evil. *Humankind creates negativity, not God.*

If God's creations are interpreted as a *part* of God, then some may feel that God has negativity within Him. But the Godhead simply has the *knowledge* of negativity. Negativity is a by-product of God's creations. Since negativity is a part of knowledge and we are the experiencing part of God, then we experience negativity and perpetrate it in order to gain wisdom from it.

God is all-loving and merciful. We, as His creations, choose to endure negativity so that we can learn more about the knowledge that the Godhead contains. Even when we experience or create this negativity, remember that it only exists in the physical world—it doesn't exist on the Other Side. If this is confusing, just keep in mind that we're only subjected to negativity while incarnate on a negative plane of unreality—for a length of time that is nothing compared to an eternity.

Maybe the following analogy will be helpful. Imagine that you created a beautiful piece of artwork. When it's done, what do you do with it? Do you proudly display it on your mantel? Do you sell it? Do you give it to a friend? Let's say, for example, that you give it to a friend. Once they receive your artwork, then your friend is responsible for what to do with it. They may proudly display it, store it in the attic, sell it, or simply throw it away. All of these actions are acceptable to God, but only you can determine which of these choices is "good" or "bad."

God has given His creations (humankind) the free will to choose all of their actions. As a result, we're responsible for ourselves, our actions, and our manner of obtaining knowledge. God has created us and allowed us to evolve on our own. He doesn't interfere in this learning process, but He constantly offers His love and support.

Yet, God has imposed one rule for all of creation. He won't allow any of His creative energy to be lost. Everything that He created is intrinsically good, but if an entity evolves into something evil or negative, they're still ultimately absorbed back into Him when they've reached their final evolvement. When and if there's a time frame involved, only God knows. All of us feel that there's no end to evolvement; it's eternal.

To summarize, we choose to experience the part of God's knowledge that is negativity. We do this to gain more knowledge about God. God is all-loving and merciful, and allows all of us to evolve on our own without His interference. Humankind created negativity in this self-evolving process. The true reality is on the Other Side—a positive dimension in which negativity doesn't exist.

How do we choose our incarnations?

Before choosing to incarnate onto the Earth plane, an entity must go through an extensive orientation process. They do this because of the vast differences between the two dimensions of positive and negative. Without orientation, they'd be totally confused and wouldn't be able to adjust without preparation.

Similarly, they go through an orientation when they come back from an incarnation—for the same reason above—and also to get over any trauma that they incurred while on the negative plane. This is conducted in what are called "Orientation Centers."

Orientation Centers were implemented because of the trauma that occurs when an entity shifts between positive and negative planes. The change is just too intense for an entity to handle. It would be comparable to traveling from a very hot, tropical climate, and then going to the North Pole without wearing any clothes! Entities on the Other Side are not subjected to negativity, and they live without it. But when they incarnate and suddenly shift to a negative plane, the resulting trauma shocks their soul. Without the process of orientation, this shock would be impossible for them to withstand.

To a lesser degree, although just as vital, is the procedure for returning from the negative plane to the Other Side. Entities who experience a traumatic death often need orientation to realize their death and prepare for their new plane of existence. Their physical life will be "reviewed" in an Orientation Center to determine if they've accomplished their goals, how well they succeeded, ways they could have improved, or any mistakes they might have made. This process gives the entity the complete scope of experience and accomplishments during their recent incarnation for their soul's evolvement.

Each quadrant has an Orientation Center. These centers are larger in some quadrants than others due to population density. All of them are amply equipped to handle any entity going to or coming from the Earth plane.

Most people regard death, or passing over, as a trauma. On the Other Side, the opposite is true—incarnating on the Earth plane is the real trauma. To prepare, each entity enters their respective Orientation Center for the quadrant where they'll incarnate.

When an entity decides to incarnate on the Earth plane, they immediately seek the help and aid of counselors at the Orientation Center. Here, they review what they want to accomplish. Depending on their needs and desires, the entity chooses parents, location, ethnic or racial group, family background, class or mode of living, body shape, appearance, health issues, environment, and conditions for positive and negative experiences. All of these factors and more are examined thoroughly by the entity and the counselors—experts on incarnation and entity needs.

Oftentimes, a counselor will try to dissuade an entity from picking an incarnation if they feel that they can't handle it. Most of the time, however, counselors help an entity choose a life that will follow their theme (such as a "major" in college), so they can evolve at their own pace in their chosen field of knowledge. Counselors are usually fifth- and sixth-level entities who are very knowledgeable about the Earth plane and what it has to offer. When I'm not aiding Sylvia, I help war victims in the Orientation Center on my home quadrant. I also assist many small children through the orientation process.

Entities can always choose their incarnations and surrounding environment. Most of their free will is implemented while they're on the Other Side. On the Earth plane, they may think they're acting with free will, but they're actually following their own subconscious knowledge and direction. Since they've pre-chosen what they want to experience on the Earth plane, their incarnation is ultimately a matter of implementing these choices.

An entity has no conscious knowledge of these predetermined elements and events. When they go through a particularly difficult time, the last thing they think about is the fact that they *chose* to go through it. Everything that they've experienced in their life is directly attributable to the choices they've made before they incarnated—whether good or bad. Some of them may take solace in this; others may not.

It's hard for a parent to realize this when they've just lost a child. Yet every member of that family chose to go through that particular experience. Those entities who feel tremendous guilt over a particular action must realize that unless it was done with malicious intent, there can be no guilt. Those entities involved chose to go through it.

Due to the orientation process, almost all entities make a smooth transition from one plane to another. There are very few "Earthbounds"—entities who don't make the transition from the Earth plane to the Other Side. They reside in a sort of "limbo" state between the two dimensions, and many times are referred to as "ghosts."

When an entity's soul enters a new fetus, and they feel that it's not the proper time or circumstance, they may exit early and come back to the Other Side. This is one of the primary reasons for miscarriages and sudden infant death syndrome (SIDS). This doesn't apply, however, to suicide.

The only action that is not charted is suicide. If an entity takes their own life, they must come back into another life immediately. Moreover, they have to come back and experience the same circumstances again. They must finish out their spiritual plan before they can stay "Home." There's no easy way out.

Orientation Centers on the Other Side are very efficient. Each provides counselors who specialize in certain types of death—cancer, suicide, trauma, war-related deaths, children's deaths, and so on. In addition, orientation areas are set aside for entities who have certain preconceived beliefs about what happens after death. This ensures that a professed atheist or a person with a traditional religious background doesn't get confused when confronted with the reality of death and the Other Side.

Francine, please tell us about your life on the Other Side.

Most of my time is devoted to guiding Sylvia and watching her loved ones. I also spend a lot of time researching my communication to those of you on the Earth plane when I speak through Sylvia's body in a trance session.

Like most other entities on the Other Side, I spend the rest of my time going to lectures, concerts, parties, and social gatherings with friends.

Compared to a normal lifestyle on the Other Side, it can be somewhat confining to be the control for a medium such as Sylvia. But again, the span of Sylvia's life on the Earth plane seems so much longer than on the Other Side.

I socialize with my friends as much as possible and often consult with Raheim (Sylvia's other spirit guide), the elders, and Jesus about Sylvia and her life's work. I keep in touch with the latest discoveries in science and the arts—and especially with those developments that deal with the Earth plane. I need to do this in order to answer questions and deal with the various problems faced by entities who are now incarnated.

When I finish my job as Sylvia's guide, I'll go back to a normal lifestyle. I'll continue to work in the Orientation Center since that's one of my primary functions on the Other Side.

I've chosen to evolve and perfect my soul by doing work on the Other Side, rather than having a large number of incarnations. It's a somewhat slower evolution process, but then, I have an eternity to fulfill it. I don't like to incarnate (as most entities I know do); therefore, I have to work and learn about negativity by associating myself with it—such as being Sylvia's guide and being somewhat "humanized" to better relate to those I serve.

To Conclude . . .

The information that I've given you about the "Other Side" is for a purpose. It's part of my function as a guide for the medium, Sylvia Browne. I've been given the responsibility to communicate truth to your plane and to help as many of you as I can—with the knowledge that there's a purpose for your existence; and that God loves you, watches over you, and created you as a part of Himself.

Most of you will accept this information, take it to heart, and utilize it. You're the lucky ones; you know truth when confronted with it. You accept it and use it for yourself and others. You gain knowledge that will help you survive your realm of negativity, and you can understand its purpose. You do nothing but gain spirituality for your own chosen level of evolvement, for you're the ones who must share the responsibility of giving this knowledge to others who don't have it. You'll do this because you're the entities who are more evolved, more loving, and more representative of God's image. *You'll do this because it's truth.*

For those of you who absolutely don't believe in the information presented to you in these chapters, try to keep an open mind. Even if you can't accept most of it, turn to logic rather than belief systems that have programmed and hampered your quest for truth. I say this not to convert you, but to make it easier for you. I have an advantage over you: I *know* it's truth. I know that you'll be confronted with it and won't be able to refute it when the time comes to make the transition to the Other Side. You'll know then that it's truth, and perhaps you'll be somewhat sad that you didn't accept it while you were incarnate. Don't be discouraged—we all evolve according to the plan that the "God within" has chosen.

§ § § ℰ ℰ ℰ

𝒫𝑎𝑟𝑡 III

REINCARNATION

The Beginnings

The belief in reincarnation is as old as the origins of humankind, especially since the concept of "rebirth" is so evident and prominent in nature. The sun is "reborn" every day after "dying" at sunset. The seasons come and go, but they always return to the beginning of their cycle. Nature is a great teacher— provoking primitive peoples to emulate and incorporate it into their many beliefs and rituals.

As humans evolved and their thought processes became more complex, so too did their belief in reincarnation. Reincarnation means something entirely different to a Hindu than it would to a Muslim or a

Christian. The reincarnation philosophy for Buddhists also varies from that of a follower of Confucius. These differences are primarily dogmatic, however. Culture, religion, ritual, and tradition all influence the entire concept of reincarnation.

If you've researched reincarnation at all, you've probably realized that most of the differences in beliefs are minor—with a few exceptions, of course. The basic premises are similar for most cultures, and the one fact that seems to unite all religions and cultures is this: *More than two-thirds of the people in this world believe in reincarnation in one form or another!*

So, why does the majority of the world's population believe in reincarnation? Is it because of religion, culture, or tradition? Does it stem from primitive human beings' innate beliefs? What is it within human beings that makes them believe in reincarnation?

I (Francine) believe that the answer is: *truth.* As you read this section, I think that most of you will see the logic behind it. I've tried to simplify and explain fully, in a logical sequence, the concept of reincarnation. In many areas, my views might conflict with existing dogma on the subject, but I happen to believe that the following material is not only the most comprehensive explanation of the many facets of reincarnation, but is also the truest interpretation in existence today.

The Purpose of Reincarnation

In simple terms, the purpose of reincarnation is to perfect the soul by gaining experience and knowledge in a physical environment. Your Earth is one such place to accomplish this. You know that you need air to breathe, food to eat, and shelter to protect yourselves from the rigors of nature. You know that you share this world with billions of other life-forms that help you to survive. You know that your world basically consists of earth and water, also used for survival. Finally, you know that humans all experience both positive and negative life situations.

The physical world is a learning place for your soul. Only there can you experience negative events and trauma. Only there can your soul test its strength by coming face-to-face with hardship. Only there can you feel alone, afraid, and abandoned. But in truth, God is ever-present with you, as the following pages will explain.

Why do we need to incarnate?

It is a natural law of progression to incarnate. In other words, we become aware that the time has come to "go to school." Since the Other Side is a perfect environment without negativity, a "physical plane" was created so that we could experience and learn about negative forces.

In all honesty, some souls never incarnate. Consequently, their climb to perfection is slow and tedious because they can't perfect in an environment that is without flaws. It takes them much longer because they can't experience the negative; they can only observe it. Their souls haven't been "tested" by negativity.

On the other hand, there are a few souls who reincarnate every century. They truly desire the highest degree of experience. There are some entities—the rare exceptions—who never choose to stay on the Other Side for any length of time. They're constantly revolving into lives. To most of us who have evolved, we find this very depressing.

Do we set a goal for our perfection?

Yes, most definitely. Each entity chooses a major theme to perfect, along with two or three subthemes in addition to the main theme. This would be comparable to taking a major and minor field of study in college. We specialize in a particular theme that branches out into other related areas. We are what you might call "specialists," because we're all individuals, but we experience different aspects of life and negativity. This, of course, holds true even on the Other Side, as we each select our level of knowledge and perfection.

We carry a main theme throughout all of our incarnations, even amid the different variations, environments, and situations. Naturally, this has a tremendous impact on our personalities, which we maintain throughout all of our lives here and on the Other Side.

When choosing a theme, we also select the amount of knowledge we wish to obtain during the fulfillment of this theme. Again, we can compare this to students who want to attain a Ph.D., while others are quite satisfied with a high school diploma. In picking a theme, we may only want to experience part of it, or as much as is humanly possible.

Themes can be defined as a "reference point" of experience, or a "frame of mind" that influences all experiences. There are 45 themes that we can choose from [see pages 104 to 114 of *Soul's Perfection* for the entire list]. I've often been asked, Why 45? The number doesn't matter as long as the totality of experience is fulfilled. From the beginning of reincarnation, we've incarnated in these select themes, and no new ones have been added or are even needed.

In all cases, incarnations are chosen for the sole purpose of achieving a goal. In most cases, this goal is to obtain knowledge. Some of us may choose to live a life to help another person in their perfection, while a select few may do so because of a karmic tie or debt. In every case, some-thing is always learned which, in turn, progresses the soul.

Since we incarnate to perfect, who judges our degree of evolvement?

You do. You're the one who knows what you most need to learn. When you're on my side, you're much more aware of your positive qualities as well as your shortcomings. A genius on your plane may use one-tenth of their mind's capacity, but when you're on the Other Side, you use nine-tenths of your capacity. You have complete awareness of where you've been and where you're going, and you're not confused or unaware. Your knowledge is vast because you can remember not only all of your past incarnations, but you also retain all of the knowledge that you've obtained while working and living on the Other Side.

This knowledge is embedded in your subconscious while you're on the Earth plane, and it opens up fully when you pass over to the Other Side. Here, you have full comprehension of how far your soul has progressed to the level of perfection you've chosen. No one is look-ing over your shoulder. You're responsible for your own learning process, just as you're responsible for attaining your chosen level of perfection. If one entity chooses a perfection level that is similar to another entity, this doesn't mean that they'll both necessarily choose the same road to attain it. You may select many lives to accomplish things that others might complete in just a few lives. It's your choice, and it doesn't matter how you do it or how long it takes.

Each of you has a part of God within you; therefore, when you judge yourself, it's essentially God who is judging Himself. The judgment process doesn't arbitrate between good and evil, as many religions have taught us. It's more of an evaluation of how you're progressing. There's no one such as St. Peter or anyone else who's going to condemn you for your actions. If you live a life that wasn't particularly successful, you and you alone will make the decision to live another life to see if you can do better. Part of the reason why reincarnation exists is to give you as many chances as you need to learn a difficult lesson. The full concept of perfection is neverending; you continue to learn even after you stop incarnating.

Does everyone evolve to a perfected state?

All of us who have chosen to perfect and experience for God will reach our chosen level of perfection. Some of us may take longer than others, but we all make it.

There's no such thing as a person who can't reach their chosen level.

If this is the case, then why do some people seem so unevolved? We can't judge a person's soul, although we do have access to records on my side, so we can more fully evaluate the progress of a particular entity. But many times we make the mistake of judging a person's behavior and we say they're not evolved. Behavior alone is not an accurate criterion for evolvement. Many of us choose lives where we become pawns for someone else's quest for perfection. We incarnate to create a certain situation or environment for someone else. On the Earth plane, every victim has to have a victimizer, every follower has to have a leader, and every "good" has to have a "bad."

Does reincarnation ever end?

You must realize that we're all here to help each other. We all want to end reincarnation so that we don't have to live with negativity, even if it's only for a fraction of eternity. It will end, however, when everyone has attained the amount of knowledge and perfection that they ordained for themselves. When all of us have sufficiently been exposed to, and learned from, the negative forces, reincarnation will cease. By helping each other attain perfection, it will end more quickly.

According to records on my side, and if everything progresses as it should, reincarnation on Earth should end by the year 2100. This doesn't preclude the fact that reincarnation will still exist on other planets, because there are billions of planets that have had or still have the capability for reincarnation. When all of the planets have evolved to the point where reincarnation is no longer necessary, then it will end.

Why do we forget our past lives?

When we incarnate, we lose all conscious memory of where we came from, what it's like, and what we've done. Conscious knowledge of our past could hinder us; it might divert us from our current path. It could also hold us back. Words cannot describe the beauty, peace, and happiness on my side: beyond description. If we retained that knowledge consciously and knew we had a choice between living in a beautiful paradise or a "slum" of negativity, most of us would be jumping off bridges to get back Home!

There are, however, several entities on the Earth side who remember bits and pieces of their past. This is referred to as "subconscious seepage," since the memory of one's past and the Other Side is buried in the subconscious mind. Some of us might "know" or suspect that we've lived before in another life—probably in another country, time, and racial or ethnic situation. We might see past-life vignettes in our dreams, or experience "déjà vu" when we visit certain places. Since our own subconscious mind has so much knowledge, there are bound to be a few leaks from time to time. Many of us, however, don't recognize them.

There are several evolved entities in the incarnate state who remember past lives and readily accept the Other Side because of it. Most of us don't remember, and we really aren't meant to. We choose a life to learn and perfect—to make the task harder and to evolve more quickly—and we choose not to have full memory so that we can learn our lessons "the hard way." We've found that these lessons have a deeper meaning and influence on our soul.

This doesn't mean that the remembrance of past lives and the Other Side is detrimental; in fact, many times it can be beneficial and help us evolve faster. Regardless of how much we remember from our subconscious, there's a built-in regulator that won't allow complete access to the Other Side. If some people have a memory of their past, they're only able to see a very small segment of it.

Do previous lives influence our current life?

Most definitely they do, although most of you don't realize it. Your likes and dislikes in this life are influenced by previous lives. Your personality has been deeply affected and built upon previous incarnations. Other areas that your past lives can tremendously influence include: physical health, appearance, race, creed, religion, value systems, wealth, habits, aesthetic talents of any kind, sex, and I could go on and on, but I think you get the general idea. Everything in your current life is affected by your past lives.

In many cases, negativity on the Earth plane is perpetuated by the influence of past lives. Bigotry and racial hatred are prime examples. Almost everyone at one time or another has experienced such prejudices—with some of you even functioning as both victim *and* offender.

Take a look at your life and analyze it as an incarnate. You can discover how many of your interests, habits, likes, and dislikes could be the direct result of a past life. Is your house furnished in a particular decor? Do you like certain foods more than others? Do you vacation in a certain place all of the time? Are you uncomfortable with a certain ethnic group? You may be surprised to learn how much influence the past can have on your life.

Is there any real benefit to remembering past lives?

For the majority of you, I would say yes. The main benefit is therapeutic in nature, but unfortunately, most therapists who practice today don't incorporate the premise of reincarnation into their methodology. Consequently, they bypass one of the primary healing modes—to relieve both physical and mental problems—for individuals: past-life therapy.

Past-life therapy, through the use of hypnotic regression, has garnered some astounding results from those who utilize it. Sylvia has used it many times and effected wellness (in one particular session) with clients who have been in psychoanalysis or medical treatment for years.

Most phobias that have no reason to exist or can't be traced to an incident in someone's current life are usually the result of a past-life experience. In fact, many traumatic incidents that a person has gone through in previous lives can be triggered by similar circumstances in their current life. Many illnesses, which doctors term "psychosomatic," are often "carried over" from past incarnations.

For example, at a certain age, a famous actor started experiencing acute pain in the solar plexus region of his body. After seeing numerous doctors, none of them could find a reason for the pain, so he consulted a psychic. The psychic determined that this actor had been "run through" with a sword in that particular area of his body during a past life. Once he discovered this, the actor no longer experienced any pain. This is a key example of how a "carryover" from a past life can affect you.

To develop your recollection of past lives, hypnosis is considered the safest and most valid method. Sylvia's church has many professional hypnotists who conduct past-life regressions. Almost everyone who undergoes past-life regression feels better mentally and physically afterward, but if you take part in this process, be prepared for an emotional release. Some of the issues you can resolve from this method are: psychosomatic ills, phobias, habits, a misguided life purpose, questions about your themes, relationship troubles, and many more. The benefits are many, although this isn't for everyone.

What is transmigration?

Transmigration is the belief that, after death, your soul can pass into any type of body, from the lowest form of life—such as an insect—to a human being. If you lived a "bad" life, you're placed into a lower form of life, depending upon the depth of your evil. If you led a "good" life, your soul will be placed into an elevated form—human.

Do we incarnate as animals or other life-forms?

No. Species remain pure to species. At the origin of reincarnation, we observed "lower" life-forms evolve in their own dimension. This discovery transpired due to personal interest, care, and the pursuit of knowledge; it was purely research. Some of us even went to the extent of "sharing" in the life forces of plants and animals (similar to the way I do when Sylvia goes into a trance). Since no one could sustain this "sharing" with lower life-forms for any length of time, the practice was soon halted. Perhaps, the knowledge of this sharing "leaked" from the subconscious mind and started the entire philosophy of transmigration.

In any case, all forms of life remain true to species. Humans incarnate only as human beings, and not as other life-forms such as animals or plants. These have their own "souls," so to speak, but they don't participate in reincarnation. When animals die, they pass over to my side and reside in areas designated for them. Plants, as a part of nature, are generally duplicated on the Other Side.

What is karma?

My definition of karma is very simple: experience. Karma is nothing more than the experience you gain while incarnate. Unfortunately, many people on the Earth plane interpret karma as negative "payback" for evil actions.

Eastern philosophies view karma as an external balance. If you live a good life and perform good deeds, you'll advance your soul by generating "good karma." If your actions are immoral, you'll incur "bad karma" or a "karmic debt," which will hamper your soul's progression. In this context, karmic debt contributes greatly to the belief of transmigration.

Karma, when viewed as a punishment, can be very harsh and unreasonable. It then becomes the equivalent of the Christian "hell," which is simply a fear tactic for control. Karma, to many, is so strictly interpreted that some people won't interfere in another person's life no matter what the circumstances. This can lead to tragedies that could have easily been avoided.

The true interpretation of karma is simply . . . your experiences in life. It shouldn't prevent you from helping others, nor should you incur karmic debt except in very rare circumstances. Experience is necessary in order for the soul to progress and learn. The whole purpose of reincarnation is to face negativity, survive it, and learn from it so that the soul can fully appreciate and know what it means to be good.

Does karma ever end?

Yes. Since karma is nothing more than experience, when all souls are finished with physical life, then the entire Earth plane will cease to exist. There will be no need for negativity to exist anymore since it has been fully experienced. When the need for negativity ceases, then the physical planes of existence will end as they will no longer be needed.

What is karmic debt?

Karmic debt is a form of retribution. When a soul causes harm to another soul, then they'll have to face reciprocation for the action. For example, if an entity murders someone, then they, in turn, would be murdered, whether it be in the same life or another.

In actuality, very few karmic debts are ever incurred. They do happen from time to time, but they're almost nonexistent. But then, you might ask, "But what about all of the atrocities committed in this world? Do entities who commit these offenses incur retribution in any way?"

The answer is yes, but retribution is not delivered on an individual basis. In the fullness of God's time, all entities who perpetuate evil shall be reabsorbed into the Godhead. However, such evildoers are necessary for the rest of us to learn from. In the short span of physical life, these entities are needed to test the strength of our soul.

A karmic debt is incurred only in cases where an entity maliciously intends to cause harm. Atrocities are committed every day, but most of these acts are not intentional. Rather, they're caused by passion, belief (political, religious, and so on), or mental derangement (caused by insanity, drunkenness, drug abuse, et cetera). Very few entities ever want to maliciously harm another entity.

In the rare case of a karmic debt, the offending entity would simply experience a similar action done to them. The purpose of this retribution is not for "punishment," but to help the entity learn the full impact of their action so that they don't repeat it.

What are karmic ties?

The term *karmic tie* is used to express a bond between entities who share past experiences or situations—whether good or bad. As few as two entities, or as many as millions, can have a karmic tie. Karmic ties are based on a number of things—love, hate, ethnic and religious backgrounds, friendship, and unfinished business.

Many of us have at least one karmic tie, and some of us have many more. Did you ever wonder why you have such an affinity (or dislike) for another person? Many times, it's because you're karmically tied to this person in some way. Let's say that an entity has an intense dislike for another entity, yet they feel drawn toward them, regardless of the disdain. If the Akashic Records were consulted, it might be discovered that these entities had lived together in a previous incarnation, developed a poor relationship, and died before working out the problems between them. Therefore, the current dislike was caused by the previous poor relationship, but the attraction was the result of the unfinished business.

Is there actually proof of reincarnation?

I would like to answer this with another question: Is there actually proof that reincarnation *doesn't* exist? This question poses a greater problem for the skeptic than the believer. Proof is intangible. When you research and do your homework on the existence of reincarnation, you'll find that there's much more "proof" *for* it than *against* it.

If you establish your case on the laws of probability, then the existence of reincarnation would triumph because more than two-thirds of the world believe in it. If you base your argument on historical documents, then you'll find that there are many references to reincarnation, particularly in the Bible. If you predicate your findings on logic, then there's no contest: Reincarnation is more logical than any other opposing viewpoint. If you strictly rely on religion as your basis for a conclusion, then the argument for reincarnation wins again, because it's either believed wholeheartedly, or at least, tolerated by the vast majority of the world's populace.

When substantiated by historical documents, the case for the existence of reincarnation has far more followers than opponents. All of the major religious writings mention reincarnation. None of them, including the Bible, ever state that reincarnation, or the belief that it exists, is false. The vast majority of famous authors have written about reincarnation; few have not. The *Dead Sea Scrolls,* and writings by the Essenes (an early gnostic sect), are making modern-day Christianity take notice in reanalyzing their theological teachings. These scribes were reincarnationists. Early writings on reincarnation were composed as far back as 2500 B.C. in China. Other writings, such those in Egypt in 3500 B.C., or in China as far back as 4500 B.C., all predate the earliest records of Judaism from which Christianity sprung.

Great philosophers and writers—such as Socrates, Aristotle, Plato, Pythagoras, Lao-tze, Chang-tze, and

Plotinus—all believed in reincarnation. Christian theologians—including St. Augustine, St. Clement, Origen, Basilides, Christian apologist Tatian, Valentinus, the manes, St. Jerome, Porphyry, St. Pamphilius, Iamblichus, Athenagoras, and St. Gregory—are just a few of the legions who believed in reincarnation. The Nag-Hammadi scrolls indicate that Jesus was either an Essene, a student of the Essenes, or at least associated very closely with this sect (which was said to have believed in reincarnation) during the "lost" or "silent" years of his life between the ages of 12 and 30. All of this evidence supports the argument *for* reincarnation, rather than *against* it.

If you base your case on logic, the existence of reincarnation prevails. Reincarnation furnishes us with very logical explanations for the inequities in life. Why is one person born poor, and another rich? Why does one person die young as opposed to another who lives a long life? Why is one person crippled, and another whole? I could go on and on. The existence of reincarnation offers a reason for these injustices because it presents the case that there's more than one life to live.

If God is all-loving and all-merciful (the basic teaching of Jesus Christ), then why does evil exist? Negativity can't survive when you know that through God's loving and merciful nature, He allows you to incarnate more than once to perfect your soul. You can then experience a life in which you're rich, poor, crippled, whole, young, or old. Logically, reincarnation doesn't detract from the teachings of Jesus; it augments them. God doesn't care how long it takes or how many lives you must live to perfect. He only wants you to achieve the ultimate goal—the perfection of your own soul.

If the argument against the existence of reincarnation is based on religion, then the nonbelievers are not well informed. All of the Eastern religions support reincarnation, and Western religions are changing their views rapidly. Nowadays, most Christians either believe in reincarnation or tolerate it because in no way does it detract from their teachings. In fact, it actually broadens them.

If you research the early Christian church, you'll find that almost all of the references to reincarnation in the Bible were expunged by the fourth century. This was an act of humankind, not God; regardless of this attempt to eradicate reincarnation, almost every Christian gnostic sect still believed in it. These sects, in turn, were literally "wiped out" by the early Church. The history of the Christian Church is filled with murder, bloodshed, and torture. (The Holy Inquisition is a prime example.) The early Christians, who believed in reincarnation, were much more loving and understanding than the "warlike" Church rulers of the Middle Ages.

Despite the many arguments disputing its existence, reincarnation seems to have the upper hand—truth always

CONVERSATIONS WITH THE OTHER SIDE

surfaces in the end. If skeptics argue with you, ask them to research reincarnation and try to prove it doesn't exist. They can investigate endlessly, but they won't find any true evidence against it. It won't matter, though, because in their search, they'll find tomes of overwhelming validation that it is, in fact, *truth*.

Do we incarnate in the opposite sex?

Each soul is innately created male or female. You all have a gender. When you incarnate, you generally manifest the same sexual gender that you are. Almost every soul, however, chooses one or two lives in the opposite sex to help round off the totality of their experience.

Many times an incarnation in the opposite sex can create confusion. This is one of the leading causes of homosexuality. Imagine, if you can, that you have the mind, emotions, and thoughts of a female, yet you have the body of a male. This can be somewhat traumatic and stressful. This is also true in the opposite case when a male incarnates in a female body.

Not every entity who incarnates in the opposite sex necessarily becomes a homosexual. Those who don't still lead lives that can confuse their soul. For example, a woman who has tremendous drive and ambition could possibly be a male in a female body, or a man who is more effeminate in nature could very well be a female in a male body. Every situation has been experienced by most of us, but due to the stress and confusion, we usually limit our incarnations in the opposite sex.

How many lives do we live?

There is no specific number of lives that we live. Most of us choose to live between 20 and 35 lives. Nevertheless, an entity can still reach their chosen level of perfection in only a few lives. Some entities choose to live more than 35 lives, usually to carry out special missions to help other entities. We don't live thousands of lives, as some Eastern philosophies teach. The most incarnations that I've ever heard an entity take is 109, but it's actually rare for an entity to approach 70 or 80 lives.

As I stated earlier, some entities never incarnate, but this is very unusual. Everyone incarnates at one time or another. Entities who choose to live only a few lives usually elect very challenging ones because they have to pack all of their experiences into fewer incarnations. This doesn't necessarily mean that these entities are more evolved; they've just chosen to fulfill their themes more quickly.

The term *old soul* is often misused. It should only refer to an entity who has lived more lives than most. It has nothing to do with the time an entity was created, especially since, according to God, all entities were created at the same time.

Regardless of the number of incarnations, the most significant achievement for us is the evolvement of the soul. We can be just as evolved as anyone else whether we've lived 20 lives or 80. It's not the number of lives we live that's important; it's what we accomplish in them.

§ § § § § §

$\mathscr{P}art$ IV

PLANNING AN INCARNATION

What kind of planning is required before we incarnate?

All entities engage in a thorough and effective planning procedure before they incarnate. No incarnation is easy—if for no other reason than crossing over into a plane of existence that runs rampant with negativity. Consequently, every entity must undergo a lengthy process in order to fully research their next incarnation. This prepares them for the ordeal ahead and helps them achieve, with the utmost success, their own perfection and progression.

When an entity decides to incarnate, they must first appear before the main Council. The Council consists of learned souls who act as a governing body for the Other Side. The entity outlines what they hope to accomplish and how they plan to do it; and the Council, in turn, analyzes this plan and points out anything that was overlooked. Upon approval, the entity then advances to a predetermined orientation center to receive more counseling from the master teachers. Here, the preparation truly begins—a long, tedious, and hardworking ordeal—for the incarnation must be reviewed repeatedly to cover all of the details and ensure that the goal is achieved.

Individual entities might require several master teachers who help them plan for the incarnation. While at the Orientation Center, plans for incarnation are fine-tuned to the smallest detail so that the entity fully understands their task. Upon completion of this process, which may take years in your timetable, the entity chooses the vehicle in which to incarnate and enters the next life through what you call the "birth process."

To help you fully understand the complete procedure, I'll now explain in more detail each step that an entity takes prior to an incarnation.

Knowledge of the Soul

Every entity has knowledge created innately within them. Part of this wisdom propels them to experience for their Creator, God. From the beginning of their individuality, each entity knows what they want to perfect, what their theme is, and the approximate number of lives it takes to obtain their own perfection level.

The innate knowledge within each entity drives them to incarnate. It's almost like a little bell that rings inside them and announces: "It's time to incarnate." When the soul receives this signal, they start to initiate plans for an incarnation.

One of the first things an entity does is review their past history, not only their prior incarnations, but their entire existence from initial creation. This allows them to confirm their progress in the evolvement of the soul. Much of this evaluation is accomplished purely through their own memory, since it's completely open when they're on the Other Side. They also use other aids, such as scanning machines, to examine the scrolls of their past incarnations, and to explore the general history of the Earth and other planets where reincarnation is prevalent.

In the beginning of creation, all entities extensively scanned the future of all planets. When reincarnation originated, entities would survey the various eras of these planets that could possibly contain a fitting scenario for their particular perfection and theme. On Earth, some of these time periods included: the age of Atlantis, the Neanderthal age, the Golden Ages of various civilizations, the Dark Ages, the Renaissance, and the Atomic age; and each could offer various challenges and opportunities to perfect the soul.

Most entities choose to incarnate in "tumultuous times," as opposed to "quiet times," because they can perfect faster in a more negative environment. To start, they'd sit in large forums and scan various time periods on a massive information board. This data network would pause at each major epoch and highlight various opportunities for incarnations— delivering details on geographical locations, parentage, ethnic and racial backgrounds, political and economic facts, social views, and much more. From here, they'd take this information and evaluate it for their own needs. For some of the more popular eras, they'd even "bid" for various incarnation openings.

Upon reviewing the past and exploring the opportunities they need to upgrade their present level, they can now present their plans to the Council.

The Council

The Council is like a governing body for the Other Side. Their responsibilities include "approving" applications from entities who wish to incarnate. This is more of a loving and caring formality that is observed due to the combined wisdom of the elders that preside on the Council. An entity doesn't necessarily need approval to incarnate, and a few have done so without it. Most entities, however, seek the Council's wisdom to help plan their incarnation because the elders' knowledge is vast, and they're very highly evolved entities. It's like the old saying: "Two heads are better than one."

The Council's expertise and knowledge combined with an entity's knowledge promise a more successful incarnation.

The Council inspects the submitted plan in great detail. Their combined knowledge will often reveal problem areas that an entity didn't considered fully. They can also warn an entity of conceivable pitfalls, areas of concern, possible failures, events that might change the total complexion of the plan, and the complexities of having a free will. In disclosing these suggestions, the Council is very nurturing. Their wisdom encourages an entity to revise their plans and consider all of the contingencies.

Many times, the Council will warn an entity about a particular incarnation. The entity is lectured extensively, cautioned about entering a life that is too horrendous, or is too much to handle. They might propose taking two or three lives to accomplish what they've planned for just one. Some entities won't listen and will argue with the Council, thinking they're justified. The elders then take a passive stand, because an entity's free will allows them to incarnate regardless of what the Council recommends. I can truly say, however, that I've never seen the elders misjudge any plans for an incarnation, but I've noticed many entities who make disastrous mistakes.

Most entities respect and listen to the Council's advice, and generally wait for their ultimate approval of the reincarnation plans. Once this is obtained, entities can proceed to the Orientation Center that best serves their needs. Here, they meet the master teachers and review the plan approved by the Council. This can be a time-consuming process, as the master teachers must familiarize themselves with every detail of what an entity wants to accomplish. An entity can spend years in the Orientation Center preparing for a life.

Once the entity and master teachers have studied every aspect of the planned incarnation, they can begin to search—with the aid of a computer-like apparatus—for the right parents, the right body, the right geographical location, the right job, any defects they're going to have, the right childhood, when they're going to die, and so on. Do they want to be rich or poor? Do they want a parent who will be a matriarch or a patriarch? Do they want parents who will be loving, divorced, or killed? Do they want brothers or sisters? How many? Do they want to marry? How many times? What kind of marriage partner do they seek? Do they want to be widowed or divorced? How many children do they want? What sex and disposition do they want for their children? How many grandchildren would they like? How many jobs would they like to pursue? How much schooling or education do they need? What are their choices for friends, relationships, traumas to be incurred, or negativity to endure? Will they be religious? Nonreligious? Which religion will they choose? Will they embrace many religions? The choices are many, and every detail is reviewed, debated, and discussed.

After finalizing the basic plan, the entity and master teachers begin to view the major events of this incarnation on a device we call "the scanner" (similar to a closed-circuit television). They actually observe the major events and choices that they've planned, gauge their reactions, and analyze their emotional response. The entity repeats this stage over and over again, incorporating possible changes due to choices exercised by other people they may encounter. For example, an entity might look at a particular event in 100 different ways to ensure that another person's actions won't hinder their goal. So, not only is their original plan scrutinized, but alternate scenarios are also rehearsed in case there was any deviation from their original path.

At this juncture, an entity now travels down through a tunnel and enters a vehicle—their mother—in the planned incarnation. It's here, and up until the time they reach the age of four, that they have the opportunity to exit. This four-year period allows their soul to acclimate to the negative plane of Earth. If they experience a drastic change from their expectations or they simply can't acclimate, then they'll exit. This is why so many mothers have miscarriages and why children die so young. The soul realizes that circumstances won't allow their plan to succeed, so they exit back Home.

In scanning an incarnation, there are millions of trails that a person could follow, but there's always the "blue track"—the most favorable path for accomplishing their goals. Other roads extend in many different directions, but they usually all lead back to the main blue track.

If, for some reason, an entity veers off of the blue track, it may be due to some type of derangement, which can make an entity feel like they're under extreme stress and pressure. This can lead to destructive behavior such as alcoholism, drug abuse, or in extreme cases, suicide. All of these possibilities are covered by the master teachers at the Orientation Center.

During the planning process, an entity is rigorously instructed to handle stress and anxiety. In most cases, they survive, but they won't remain on the blue track. This is the primary reason for the extensive planning, constant review, and programming of the subconscious mind: to survive the incarnation and accomplish everything in the plan.

When all of the planning, counseling, and programming is finished, the entity then incarnates. The entire plan for the incarnation is in the entity's subconscious mind, and the spirit guides watch over them as they live their lives.

How do we find the people and the situations we need for our perfection?

The population and diversity of lifestyles on Earth allows for almost any situation you might want to choose for your perfection. You can incarnate into the most primitive or the most advanced cultures. You can be an executive in a New York City skyscraper or a pygmy in Africa. Whatever situation you desire, there's a place that fits your reincarnation plan fully.

What if several entities choose the same parent at the same time?

This is a very rare occurrence, but it can happen. When it does, the Council will review all plans submitted for the same incarnation scenario. Then they'll make a decision based on merit, and award the situation to the entity who will garner the most from the incarnation. There are no hard feelings or recriminations, as all entities know that the Council is doing its best for all involved. Every effort is then made to find a similar situation for the other entities.

Do we make contracts with other people before an incarnation?

Most incarnations are planned years in advance so that all entities involved are subconsciously aware of the major events and influences in their lives. When an entity enters into an incarnation, a huge chain of lives is linked together, and each one is aware of the others.

For example, when you plan a life, the entities you've chosen as parents haven't incarnated, yet you meet them on my side and go over all of your plans as well as theirs, thus creating a "contract to incarnate together." You do this with all of the major entities who will influence your planned incarnation. It's not unusual for an entity to meet with several generations of a family, making sure that the scenario planned will evolve and exist by the time the incarnation takes place.

In cases where less time is devoted to planning an incarnation, entities know what to expect, even though they haven't conferred with everyone involved. For example, you could incarnate without knowing exactly who will incarnate as your son. But you know that this entity will fit into your overall plan that incorporates what your son will be like. This happens infrequently, but it's not unusual.

Perhaps the most significant "contract" that you make before an incarnation is with your spirit guide. While on the Other Side, you choose a friend or someone you respect and have confidence in to become your spirit guide. This is a serious and significant choice because the spirit guide must know all of your plans and try to guide you through the events so that you accomplish everything planned. If, for some reason, you go "off track" in life, they try to bring you back or at least help you fulfill most of what you want to accomplish. They observe all of your actions and help you evaluate your life when you pass over to my side. The devotion and efforts of a spirit guide are happily provided, as they all wish to help everyone achieve their perfection.

What is the birth process like?

Before an entity incarnates, they enter into what we call the "Hall of Wisdom." This is a very beautiful building, constructed like the Greek Parthenon, with pink marble everywhere. Here, an entity composes themselves for the ordeal of life. They meditate and examine their planned life once again with the master teachers. You must realize that most entities who incarnate really don't like to do so, because it means leaving the positive reality and moving into a plane of negativity where they lose their conscious memory of Home. It's not a pleasant experience.

Upon completion of any last-minute preparations in the Hall of Wisdom, we enter into a vaporlike tunnel—a bridge between the two dimensions—the Earth plane and the Other Side. Whether entering into a new body or leaving an old body after physical death, we use this passageway to transcend from one dimension to another. The tunnel is like a vortex or a void, which is sometimes quite dark but has a light at the end of it. When we enter, we feel a wind rushing by us—not a powerful wind—but a gentle, brisk breeze.

As we move through the tunnel and into a new body, conscious memory starts to fade. Many of us try to keep our thoughts intact, but none of us have been successful. This passageway can be somewhat frightening, although the master teachers try to fully prepare us for the experience.

Since thoughts are things, and we can transport ourselves with thought, we've already located the vehicle (body of the mother) into which we'll incarnate. As we move through the tunnel, we begin in a very solid state and then, as we move farther along, we become very etheric, almost like a "cloud mass." (It should be noted here that entities on the Other Side are more solid than human beings because they're the true reality.) At this point, like all entities, we enter the mother's body through the pituitary gland and then move into the fetus. The entire process takes no longer than two and a half minutes.

Many women have actually sensed the entering of the soul (who will become their child) into their body. They experience great emotion that is indescribable, and they even shed tears of joy as a result of this euphoric sense. The sensation is so brief, however, that most women think it's a hormonal imbalance or just a funny, fluttering feeling. But it's actually the soul entering the body and the subconscious mind acknowledging the entrance.

Most entities enter the mother's womb anywhere from four to eight months into pregnancy. The more experienced entities usually incarnate during the seventh or eighth month because waiting in the womb can be quite boring. Even though we lose most of our conscious memory in the birth process, our subconscious is functioning fully and completely. Entities waiting in the womb are much more astute than you can imagine. They readily absorb what's going on around the mother, so be careful what you say around babies, whether they're newborn or still in the womb.

One of the most severe traumas we can experience is the birth process. We begin in a warm, protected, and positive plane of existence (the Other Side), and proceed into a cramped space (the womb). From there, we're thrust into the world with its bright lights and loud noises, and there are rough hands pulling us into a cold and heavy atmosphere. Our small body feels like we're encased in lead. The physical body is the hardest thing to adapt to while incarnate. It's so much heavier in comparison to the body we have on the Other Side. The vibrational level of the Earth plane is also slower and more ponderous, so the gravity makes us feel like we're covered with cement. The birth process undoubtedly validates the fact that we're truly in a negative plane of existence.

§ § § ℰ ℰ ℰ

ॐ Part V ॐ

DO NOT JUDGE

The important thing to remember about the premise of reincarnation is not so much its intricacies, but its philosophy and reason for being. God wanted all creations to experience knowledge for Him. Wisdom encompasses both the positive and negative. Since God is all-loving and all-merciful, He created a reality of nothing but positive energy (the Other Side), in which all of His creations could reside for eternity. To help His creations learn about the negative side of experience, the Earth plane and others like it were created. This temporary plane of existence allows you to experience the negative, but only for a very short time.

Recognizing the effect of negativity on the soul, and realizing that the tremendously large body of experience couldn't be accomplished all at once, God instituted reincarnation. Since His creations must have this wisdom for the perfection of the soul, reincarnation was implemented.

However, if you could endure small doses of negativity in a positive environment with "rest periods" in between, it would be much less traumatic.

It's not easy to survive in a negative environment and it's tough to be subjected to the pain that transpires on the Earth plane. To help you understand more fully that your world has a Divine plan, know this: *The Earth is meant to be negative and will always remain negative until God disposes of it. It's the school for your soul—to learn from and experience negativity.*

It may be hard for some of you to accept the fact that the Earth plane will always be negative. You try to foster goodness in the world. You try to end suffering. You try to stop the killing of other human beings. Certainly, you do all of this. You'd be remiss in your duty to God if you didn't. You must remember, however, that it's done out of necessity. If negativity didn't exist, what would you fight against? You learn about yourself when you fight against an injustice. You view it, attack it, try to suppress it, and experience it so that you know all of its facets, all of its ways, and all of its effects.

In fighting negativity, you must be careful not to create more of it. You can't rid the Earth of the negative—it's meant to be here—but you can make your own island of Light and find others who profess the same belief. If you become too zealous in your fight against the negative, you can ultimately perpetuate it.

Do not judge! This should be your battle cry. Jesus Christ said it when the crowd wanted to stone Mary Magdalene. You can only judge yourself. No one else has the right to do so. How can anyone know the reason behind an action without recognizing the motive for it? How can anyone discern the true motive without the knowledge of the soul who committed the act? No incarnate person can perceive these things. Only entities on the Other Side can know—and only because of the Records. The subconscious mind of the entity committing the act is aware of the reason, and the only other Being who knows is God.

If a person commits an atrocity, you can judge the act—*but not the soul who committed the act.* You judge and punish negative actions so that you have some control and order in society. However, the soul of an entity can't be judged.

Let's say that an entity wants to experience the act of murder. While on the Other Side, they make a "contract" with another person, who wants to experience jail, to become their murderer. Both entities enter, and the murder is committed in its own chosen time. Society judges the entity who committed the murder and sends them to prison. Most people would judge them as a lost soul who is beyond redemption. Society did what it had to do to maintain order. The others who judged the soul as unsalvageable would be wrong.

Erroneous judging perpetuates negativity. So much bigotry and hatred have been created by prejudging other cultures and ethnic groups. So many atrocities have been committed in the name of God to save the "heathen." So many cultures have been destroyed by those who think they know more. When will it end? It will end when you stop trying to be God on Earth and refrain from judging others.

You must live your life as best as you can. You're going to make mistakes, but you'll learn from them. If you can maintain a pure motive in all of your thoughts and actions, then you'll know within your own soul that you're doing the right thing. Be a leader, not a follower. Don't let people influence you to prejudge others. Keep an open mind and heart, and embrace all souls as much as you possibly can. Simplify life by realizing that you're experiencing it for God. Do all of this and your soul will shine like a beacon for others to follow. Do all of this, and you'll fulfill your destiny and stand proudly before God when you return Home.

§ § § © © ©

§ About the Author §

Millions of people have witnessed **Sylvia Browne's** incredible psychic powers on TV shows such as *Montel Williams, Larry King Live, Entertainment Tonight,* and *Unsolved Mysteries;* she has also been profiled in *Cosmopolitan, People* magazine, and other national media. Her on-target psychic readings have helped police solve crimes, and she astounds audiences wherever she appears. Sylvia is the author of numerous books and audios; is the president of the Sylvia Browne Corporation; and is the founder of her church, the Society of Novus Spiritus, located in Campbell, California.

§ § § § § §

Contact Sylvia Browne at:
www.sylvia.org
or
Sylvia Browne Corporation
35 Dillon Ave.
Campbell, CA 95008
(408) 379-7070

Other Hay House Titles of Related Interest

BOOKS

Born to Be Together:
Love Relationships, Astrology, and the Soul,
by Terry Lamb

Colors & Numbers:
Your Personal Guide to Positive Vibrations in Daily Life,
by Louise L. Hay

The Experience of God:
How 40 Well-Known Seekers Encounter the Sacred,
edited by Jonathan Robinson

Experiencing the Soul:
Before Birth, During Life, After Death,
by Eliot Jay Rosen

Infinite Self:
33 Steps to Reclaiming Your Inner Power,
by Stuart Wilde

The Lightworker's Way:
Awakening Your Spiritual Power to Know and Heal,
by Doreen Virtue, Ph.D.

The Reconnection:
Heal Others, Heal Yourself,
by Dr. Eric Pearl

Visionseeker:
Shared Wisdom from the Place of Refuge,
by Hank Wesselman, Ph.D.

AUDIOS

Developing Your Own Psychic Powers,
by John Edward

Psychic and Intuitive Healing,
by Barbara Brennan, Rosalyn Bruyère,
and Judith Orloff, M.D., with Michael Toms

Unleashing Your Psychic Potential,
by John Edward

Notes

Notes

Notes

Notes

Notes

Notes

Notes

Notes

We hope you enjoyed this Hay House book. If you would like to receive a free catalog featuring additional Hay House books and products, or if you would like information about the Hay Foundation, please contact:

Hay House, Inc.
P.O. Box 5100
Carlsbad, CA 92018-5100

(760) 431-7695 or (800) 654-5126
(760) 431-6948 (fax) or (800) 650-5115 (fax)
www.hayhouse.com

Published and distributed in Australia by:
Hay House Australia, Ltd. • 18/36 Ralph St. • Alexandria NSW 2015
Phone: 612-9669-4299 • *Fax:* 612-9669-4144 • www.hayhouse.com.au

Published and Distributed in the United Kingdom by:
Hay House UK, Ltd. • Unit 202, Canalot Studios
222 Kensal Rd., London W10 5BN • *Phone:* 44-20-8962-1230
Fax: 44-20-8962-1239 • www.hayhouse.co.uk

Published and Distributed in the Republic of South Africa by:
Hay House SA (Pty), Ltd., P.O. Box 990, Witkoppen 2068
Phone/Fax: 2711-7012233 • orders@psdprom.co.za

Distributed in Canada by:
Raincoast • 9050 Shaughnessy St., Vancouver, B.C. V6P 6E5
Phone: (604) 323-7100 • *Fax:* (604) 323-2600

Sign up via the Hay House USA Website to receive the Hay House online newsletter and stay informed about what's going on with your favorite authors. You'll receive bimonthly announcements about: Discounts and Offers, Special Events, Product Highlights, Free Excerpts, Giveaways, and more!

Exclusive
SYLVIA BROWNE
Lecture Tape—FREE!

With one-year subscription

Fold along dotted line.